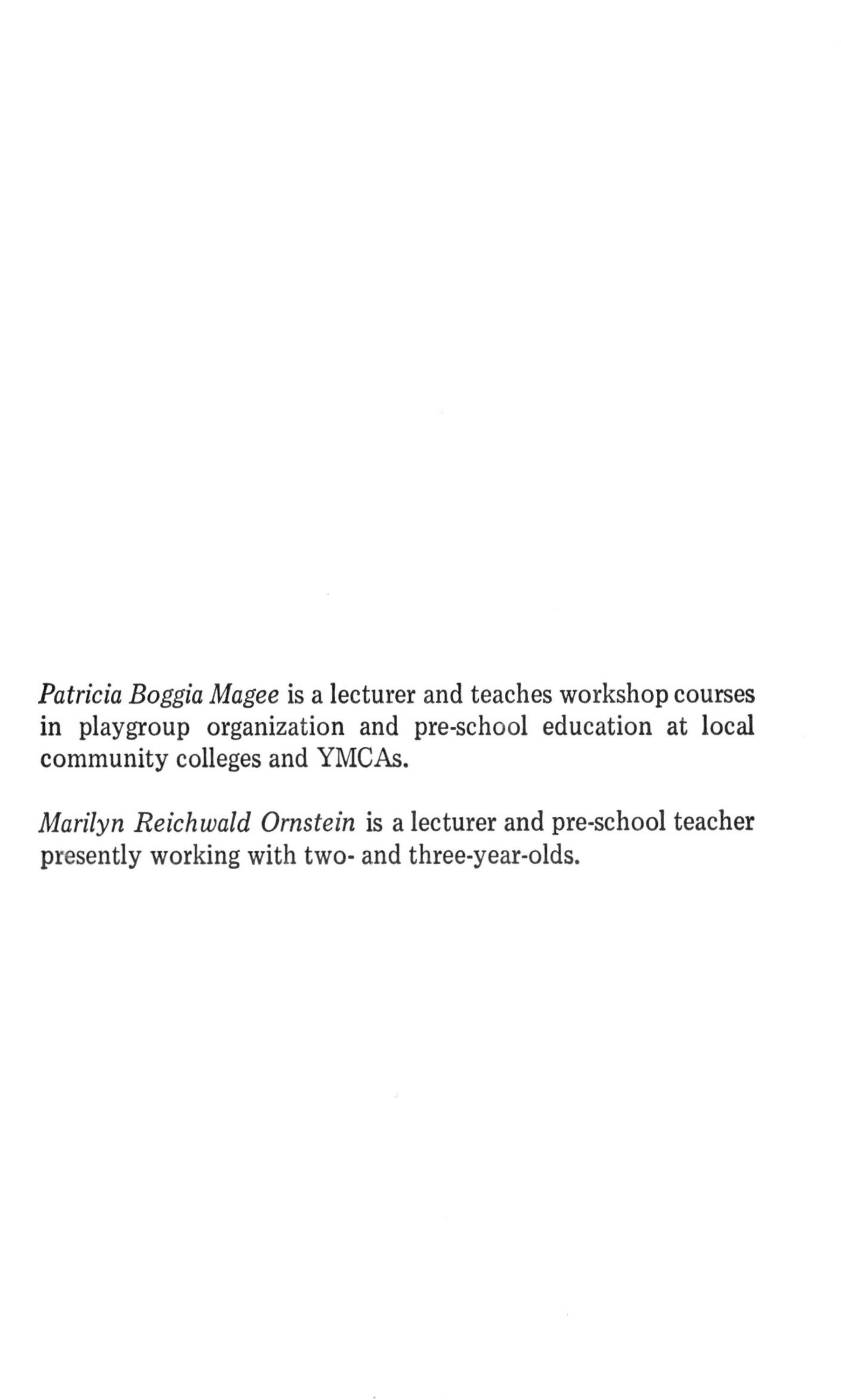

Patricia Boggia Magee is a lecturer and teaches workshop courses in playgroup organization and pre-school education at local community colleges and YMCAs.

Marilyn Reichwald Ornstein is a lecturer and pre-school teacher presently working with two- and three-year-olds.

PRENTICE-HALL INTERNATIONAL, INC., *London*
PRENTICE-HALL OF AUSTRALIA PTY. LIMITED, *Sydney*
PRENTICE-HALL OF CANADA, LTD., *Toronto*
PRENTICE-HALL OF INDIA PRIVATE LIMITED, *New Delhi*
PRENTICE-HALL OF JAPAN, INC., *Tokyo*
PRENTICE-HALL OF SOUTHEAST ASIA PTE. LTD., *Singapore*
WHITEHALL BOOKS LIMITED, *Wellington, New Zealand*

COME WITH US TO PLAYGROUP

A HANDBOOK FOR PARENTS AND TEACHERS OF YOUNG CHILDREN

Patricia Boggia Magee
Marilyn Reichwald Ornstein

PRENTICE-HALL, INC., Englewood Cliffs, New Jersey 07632

Library of Congress Cataloging in Publication Data

MAGEE, PATRICIA BOGGIA.
Come with us to playgroup.

(A Spectrum Book)
Bibliography: p.
Includes index.
1. Play groups—United States. 2. Education, Preschool—United States. I. Ornstein, Marilyn Reichwald. II. Title.
HQ782.M325 649'.5 81-10538
AACR2

ISBN 0-13-152587-5

ISBN 0-13-152579-4{PBK.}

A SPECTRUM BOOK. Printed in the United States of America.

10 9 8 7 6 5 4 3 2 1

Editorial/production supervision and interior design by Carol Smith
Cover design by Jeannette Jacobs
Interior photographs by Diane Neumier
Manufacturing buyer: Cathie Lenard

TO OUR CHILDREN, MIRIAM, NAOMI, MICHAEL, MITCHELL, MARC, AND MERIDITH, WHO HAVE BEEN OUR SOURCE OF INSPIRATION, AND TO OUR HUSBANDS, MIKE AND PETER, WHOSE SUPPORT, GOOD HUMOR, AND CONFIDENCE SUSTAINED US THROUGH OUR PROJECT

CONTENTS

PREFACE ix

1
THE PLAYGROUP EXPERIENCE: AN OVERVIEW 1

2
STARTING A PLAYGROUP:
PARTICIPANTS AND GUIDELINES 11

3
CREATING THE PHYSICAL ENVIRONMENT:
DELECTABLE COLLECTIBLES 21

4
CREATING THE SOCIAL ENVIRONMENT:
A HAPPY PLACE TO VISIT 31

5
COMMUNICATION: LET'S PRETEND 43

6
MANIPULATION AND COORDINATION:
LITTLE FINGERS BUSY AT WORK 49

7
CREATIVITY AND EXPLORATION OF MATERIALS:
THE YOUNG PICASSOS 59

8
CLASSIFICATION AND DISCRIMINATION:
THE MATCH GAME 73

9
AUDITORY SKILLS:
CAPTURING THEIR EYES AND EARS 79

10
OBSERVATION AND PARTICIPATION:
EDIBLE DELIGHTS 101

11
APPRECIATION OF THE ENVIRONMENT:
OUTDOOR ACTIVITIES AND EXCURSIONS 111

12
GRAND FINALE: SIMPLE PROJECTS
THEY'LL BE PROUD TO SHOW OFF 131

A HAPPY ENDING 139

RECOMMENDED READINGS 141

INDEX 143

PREFACE

This book was written to introduce you and your children to the concept of a playgroup. Both of us are educators of both parents and children, and it is our fondest hope that our interest in enhancing child-parent relationships through educational play—which is what playgroup is all about—will provide a source of encouragement and information for you. We have written it from an experienced viewpoint. Over the last several years we have been involved with five different playgroups. In addition, we developed an extensive questionnaire to interview many other parents involved in playgroups in various communities. The responses of these parents appear throughout the book to highlight and supplement many of our opinions. The parents who responded to our questionnaire were from diverse backgrounds. Some were home centered, some were students, some worked as volunteers, and others worked at paying jobs. Geographically they spread from Chapel Hill, North Carolina and Princeton, New Jersey (both college towns), to New York City and Greenfield, Massachusetts. The responses to our questionnaire were remarkably consistent, indicating very positive feelings about playgroups, and they were quite close to our own feelings and thoughts.

This book provides the basic background for organizing and maintaining a successful playgroup; it is written for parent and child alike since you both are the playgroup. It is meant not only to encourage an enriched child-care environment, but also to tap the hidden creativity in each of you. For those who do not wish to conduct a playgroup it remains a valuable resource. Its contents have served as background material for classes involving caretakers, nursery school teachers, students in early childhood education, parents and grandparents in search of new ideas. This book is a positive statement about your potential and the gifts you have to offer. Whoever you may be, if by reading this book you give some joy to the children you touch, then we have succeeded in our goal.

COME WITH US TO PLAYGROUP

1

THE PLAYGROUP EXPERIENCE

AN OVERVIEW

This book evolved from our initial decision to conduct a playgroup for our children. We were neighbors who moved to Chapel Hill, North Carolina at approximately the same time. Our babies, who became involved in the playgroup specifically discussed in this book, were born three weeks apart and progressed through the stages of early childhood together. We were lucky to have each other. Our respective families were great distances away, and we, along with our other family members, "adopted" each other. The lack of extended family close by is a fact of life today, and in many ways is a detriment to parenting. We were lifesavers for each other during many familiar family crises, from illnesses to dentist appointments. Anyone who has had a tooth drilled while their toddler crawled around the office knows exactly what we mean. When our older children went off to school part-time, it became clear to us that our youngest children, who were nearing two years of age, needed a situation that would provide them with peer involvement and social experiences with other children and adults.

Our young preschoolers missed their older siblings and wanted their own friends and experiences to share at the evening meal. They needed wider social contacts to continue growing in their own right and to keep up with the other family members. They were no longer babies content to play by themselves and listen while the family "action" went on around them. At the time that this need was growing in our children, both of us had expanding interests outside the home and wanted a steady and reliable amount of free time. We couldn't rely on grandparents, and finding appropriate sitters on weekdays was a constant problem, not to mention expense. When, for example, we finally found one, she turned out to be a lovely doting grandmother who did well with babies but was hardly stimulating company for active, exploring, messy preschoolers. These children needed active adult participation in their play and, more importantly, other children with whom to play. They needed someone to help guide their block-building activities, someone interested in their ever-growing verbal skills, and someone who wanted to help them grow and learn. In short, we felt that they needed a playgroup, one in which several children could get together for sessions of supervised play and exploration. Sound like an interesting child-care alternative you haven't explored? Read on and we will fill you in on the many reasons and rationales for getting a playgroup started.

WHAT IS A PLAYGROUP?

As we were outlining the book, we asked a photographer if she might consider doing a pictorial study of our "playgroup." She replied, "Sure, what time does the play begin?" So, perhaps we'd do best to start with a definition of a *playgroup.* The term applies to a child-care cooperative. Parents work together, caring for the group's children without pay. The concept has taken different forms. For some, playgroups simulate a more formal preschool in size and scope. Teachers are hired and children from ages three to five are included. The parents run and maintain the cooperative themselves and combine funds to rent a site for the group. For others, the term playgroup refers to a slightly different child-care arrangement, although the basic concept of cooperative free care is the core. For these parents, ourselves included, a playgroup is a small group of children (usually four) gathered together under the guidance of one of the parents for several mornings or afternoons of supervised play each week.

The playgroup is held in one of the parents' homes with the size of the group and the age span of the children intentionally restricted.

ADVANTAGES OF A PLAYGROUP

What about the other child-care alternatives that have developed over time? These include day-care centers, nursery schools, and private sitters. We have already discussed the issue of sitters, but what about the other options? In our view, these often fall short for some children because of the length of the day, large social setting with many children and adults to cope with, sheer expense, and lack of attention and affection due to the large teacher-child ratio. A truly good child-care center is hard to find. We explored some centers in our area, and we were frankly concerned with the child/adult ratios. The children seemed tired and unoccupied. With such large numbers of children to care for, the teachers or personnel have a difficult time attending to the children's individual needs as we would have liked. The places we visited seemed so impersonal, the settings too large for our children to cope with. A friend of ours from Flushing, New York described her reasons for choosing a playgroup over these other alternatives: "I wanted my child to be with other children with a proper program, thus a baby-sitter would not do. My daughter was too young for nursery school, nor did I want her away from me at an all-day daycare center. Playgroup was a far better program for her than any alternative. She would socialize, play, and yet still be in a constructive parent-led situation."

The playgroup concept helped us solve the dilemma many parents find themselves in today: How to balance our own lives and careers, do errands and household work, and find time to breathe, while at the same time providing our children with the companionship and the independence they need. We felt that we knew our children better than any outsider possibly could and that we had the potential to teach them many things that needed to be taught. The way to do this, and to pursue our own individual interests, seemed to be through the establishment of a playgroup.

Our solution worked. The playgroups with which we have been associated have been very successful. Has it been much trouble? Our answer is "surprisingly little." And, since the decision to be involved is a positive commitment, and the accent is on thorough preparation and high-quality fun, the anxiety level is very low. In addition, the realization that our morning of supervision will be rewarded with three or more free mornings in which to pursue our own desires, and not at the expense of our children, is reassuring indeed.

What does such a parent-run environment have to offer? Briefly it has what other alternatives don't: A limited, protected social setting for the preschooler; a parent's loving guidance and reassurance; an enriched environment for a small group of children, for an appropriate length of time; and a total cost of practically nil. One parent from Chapel Hill, North Carolina wrote: "I considered a two morning a week school but the playgroup had the advantage of a smaller size group, no money outlay, my active participation, which I found was good for me and for my son. I found separation from him hard on me. Playgroup parents were understanding and patient." A woman from Greenfield, Massachusetts wrote: "I wanted something smaller than a nursery school or day-care center and I also wanted to be involved and have more contact with children than the other settings would have provided." Simply put, a playgroup offers the satisfaction of setting aside a special time with your child and realizing that you have a tremendous hidden talent and potential waiting to be exposed by a commitment such as this.

The parents of the playgroups in which we participated received the joy of seeing their children grow verbally, manually, and socially. Indeed, our playgroup flourished. The parents fed each other's imagination, and creativity abounded with the end-

less discussions about the children and their progress. Each year ended with the feeling that we not only had enriched each other's lives, but knew and appreciated our children better. One of our playgroup parents, Ann Hoyer, now of Sanford, North Carolina, summarized the meaning of the playgroup experience so well that, with her permission, we are including her letter as written.

I wanted Jed to be part of a playgroup so that he would have an assured and predictable playtime with children his own age. I wanted his energy and eagerness and imagina-

tion, his two-year-oldness, directed toward simple, positive activities. I hoped to encourage an outgoing nature: I prayed he might learn to cooperate with other toddlers. I felt Jed was young enough that I wanted him in a home situation. I felt he was old enough to see that all homes have rules, all parents have expectations. A playgroup in a few selected homes seemed a good way to introduce him to the wondrous variations between families and parenting.

Jed developed quickly a special fondness toward his playgroup friends, and even toward playgroup days. If he was in a petulant mood I could change his tone remarkably by commenting, "Tomorrow's playgroup." Jed never cried when I left him at his friends' homes, but after a few playgroup sessions he always cried when I came to pick him up. An only child living far away from extended family, Jed made his playgroup friends "honorary cousins." Through them he lived vicariously the sibling experience. After a morning at Mitchell's he always had a "baby Marcie" story to repeat and repeat. Actually, he thought of babies as dolls; he was amazed that they could be irritable.

Jed was proud of the projects the children had worked on and brought home. His sense of mastery was hard-earned. It was as difficult for him to master listening to directions from another adult as it was for him to coordinate paper and paste. He was pleased when he was self-controlled. He enjoyed the process as much as the product. The children learned to share activities long before they could toys. It was delightful to watch four toddlers giggling among themselves as they worked.

I figured at least I'd gain free time and a guaranteed nap on playgroup days by joining a playgroup, but since Jed was my first child I didn't realize how much more than that I'd get. Planning a morning for the children turned out to be interesting and entertaining. Very soon I realized that young preschoolers accomplish much more than I'd expected. It became challenging to see what new ideas would catch the children's attention. It was surprising how quickly the kids could run through what I thought was a full morning program. Another surprise was how quickly they could run through what looked like an inexhaustible supply of apple juice.

Playgroup helped me to see other children Jed's age at close range, regularly. Their "company behavior" wore off, and as I watched their everyday personalities at work together, I developed a more realistic perspective on Jed's behavior. It was a relief to see that other children sulked and balked. Of course knowing Naomi, Glen, and Mitchell meant conceding that there could be other children as precocious and adorable as my Jed. I do believe that the time spent with other toddlers helped me deal with Jed more reasonably. I will always be glad I looked on as the four children played and worked intently. For me, and for many other parents, there may be no better opportunity to see my child at his job-school.

And lastly, as a newcomer in town, playgroup was a good chance for me to become close to other parents, parents who by choosing to do a playgroup stood out as concerned and generous in spirit. It was helpful to have these friends during those parenting crisis times. When I went to them with a problem about Jed I knew I was getting the opinion of parents who had worked with my child over many weeks. They had seen him laughing, screaming, spilling, pinching, coping and not coping. Their helpful listening, discussing, and advice were super indeed.

There is a postscript to our playgroup saga. Three of these children attended nursery school together the following year. The teacher, Caroline Lindsay, was impressed with the children who had had a playgroup experience. When we asked her for some written thoughts, she contributed the following statement:

> *I have had a number of children with playgroup experience as members of my nursery school classes. These children have already gone a long way toward solving the separation from mother crisis when they moved from the small comfortable group to the larger world of nursery school. These children have had experience with sharing toys and adult attention. They are used to group activity such as stories read to several children rather than as a one-on-one activity. They are also familiar with the use of materials. This has usually been an easy adjustment for these children and a positive help to the class because they share their knowledge with other children.*
>
> *One year I had a group of three children from one playgroup in my class. They comforted and supported each other without excluding others. They had lots of good ideas and created a climate of good group feeling for the other children in the class.*

2

STARTING A PLAYGROUP

PARTICIPANTS AND GUIDELINES

Some of our friends and parents we interviewed were hesitant about the idea of a playgroup. Some felt insecure conducting various activities, while others worried about their schedules or other commitments. Let's look at the misgivings we heard most often and see how they can be overcome.

COMMON MISGIVINGS

I'm not artistically creative. I can't really help them make anything. A nurse from New York expressed this common concern. But as she continued, she discovered her own special talents. "I'm not musical so I can't help them there either. I do love children, I can handle them well and with ease. I love to tell children stories and to cook with them as well." Another parent said, "I was a little worried at first about how I would handle and cope with five children when it was my turn. The first few times the projects were too difficult and the children were restless. But as time went on I relaxed, found my areas of strength, and the mornings were wonderful." Not everyone is a Beethoven or Picasso, we realize that, but you don't have to be. Invariably parents sell themselves short in the talent department. In our playgroup we emphasized each other's skills and talents. The result: An overall enriched program. One parent enjoyed music and another was involved in art projects. A third parent liked cooking and her large eat-in kitchen facilitated the concocting of great edible delights. Our fourth parent, with a small apartment but a large imagination and station wagon, excited the children beyond belief with fascinating excursions. Imagine your little preschoolers watching ice cream being made at a local ice cream parlor and then being treated to a cone at 10:00 A.M.

I work full-time, so I can't be in a playgroup. Yes you can, and some of the parents we interviewed over the years were. An interviewee from Greenfield, Massachusetts was a nurse who worked the late afternoon shift. She held playgroup during the morning when she was normally at home. Throughout our interviews we found that parents who were enthusiastic and wished to be involved were accommodated. In a playgroup in Chapel Hill, North Carolina a parent who worked part-time chose to take her turn on Saturday mornings. Another scheduled her time from three to five in the afternoon. This particular parent worked mornings. When she arrived home from work she had a leisurely lunchtime and rest time with her child. At 3:00 she and the child were ready for a social/playtime once again. We did our best in our own playgroup to be flexible. For example, one of us had an older child in school only on Monday, Wednesday, and Friday. We accommodated this individual's wishes by scheduling playgroup on Mondays and Wednesdays so she would be completely free for playgroup while her older child was at school. Remember, with four parents, arrangements need to be made only once a month. Two sample playgroup schedules are arranged below. Each schedule represents one month of playgroup sessions. These particular parents chose these two different ways of handling the same time allotments. Playgroup I had parents with no other work/school commitments. Playgroup II involved a part-time working mother and a mother who was a graduate student.

PLAYGROUP I

Week 1

Monday 9:30–11:30	*Parent A*
Wednesday 9:30–11:30	*Parent B*

Week 2

Monday 9:30–11:30	*Parent C*
Wednesday 9:30–11:30	*Parent D*
Week 3	*same as week 1*
Week 4	*same as week 2*

PLAYGROUP II

Week 1

Monday and Wednesday 9:30–11:30	*Parent A*

Week 2

Monday and Wednesday 9:30–11:30	*Parent B*

Week 3

Monday and Wednesday 9:30–11:30	*Parent C*

Week 4

Monday and Wednesday 9:30–11:30	*Parent D*

The playgroup schedule of Playgroup II worked well for them as it facilitated work/study time and made other child-care arrangements simpler.

One of our parents said at the end of the year, "When you asked me to join the group, I really felt inadequate to handle the situation. But I was so impressed after watching the other parents, that for the first time I made a concerted effort to gather information for preschoolers. The playgroup made me set aside a special time for my child."

And one more thing. Too often the isolated dedicated parent works day in and day out with no thank-you from child or spouse. Here's a system where thank-yous are built in. It's hard to explain the exhilaration you feel when three of your peers genuinely congratulate you on a project you worked hard to prepare. During an interview session with a group of parents in Greenfield, Massachusetts we discussed the built-in rewards of conducting a playgroup. We were impressed by the support and comradery expressed by these parents. One parent was discussing her feelings of insecurity and inadequacy concerning the handling of five children. She was immediately interrupted by a burst of comments from the others saying "Oh—you're the one that got the playgroup off to a great start. You had great things planned and the children enjoyed coming to your home so much." She responded, "Are you kidding? You were the one who was artistic—I use your ideas at home all the time." Had we not interrupted them the "backslapping" would have gone on through lunchtime. Don't we all need a little bit of encouragement like that?

What about my home? It's small, packed with expensive stuff, certainly not suitable for a whole group of children. We admit, you may have to make some changes in your environment to accommodate the children for your day. Put your older or younger child's toys away during playgroup time. While you're at it, put away that superspecial toy your own child will resist sharing. Cover that special antique chair with an old sheet. Cover good rugs with a large piece of oilcloth or plastic tablecloth that will handle occasional spills from projects or snacks. If you live on a busy street, have an unfenced yard, or live in a tenth-floor apartment, the sidewalks or a playground will do for outside play. The point is, with a little thought and preparation you can adapt. And the rewards are just stupendous.

I have a small baby, so you better count me out. Not true. One of our parents had a small baby and found that he blended in surprisingly well. Mitchell's little brother, Marc, a demanding one-year-old, was quite happy in the midst of the hustle and bustle. His mother saved quiet projects such as art or reading for Marc's nap time. At times a highly visible sleeping blanket or edible delight would be enough to allow Marc to slip off to sleep right at action central. For outdoor play, simply put the baby in a backpack, freeing your hands for swinging and helping the other children. On this one day, try not to be rigid. Relaxed, flexible parents have room for their own children as well as others.

WHERE DO YOU BEGIN?

Choosing the Participants. Your first problem may well be how to meet people to form a playgroup. A few friendly hints from those who learned the hard way. We started off by asking friends and neighbors if they knew of anyone with a young child who might be interested in starting a playgroup. When that didn't work, we posted small notices on bulletin boards at various local churches or synagogues and even considered advertising in our town newspaper. We allowed ourselves to be drawn into conversations with people at parks, community pools, or YMCA toddler classes, considering any place where people congregate with young children as a possible hunting ground for a participant. We have been a part of three separate playgroups over the past three years, and each year has differed in the way we found participants. Regardless of the method of selection, a little extra care in making your choice will ensure success.

Don't jump right in and grab a parent for your playgroup without thorough consideration. Try socializing and get a feel for the person's attitudes toward children. Be observant! Needless to say the best way to know about parent-child interactions is to spend time observing. Know in your own mind the types of interactions with which you feel comfortable. Below are a few questions you might keep in mind when selecting participants. In our selection process, keeping these things in mind gave us a guideline:

1. *Does the parent appear relaxed with his or her own child?*
2. *Does the parent seem to enjoy interacting with young children?*
3. *In discussions about various things that can be done with young children does the parent seem responsive and interested in carrying out these activities?*
4. *Does the parent exhibit a sense of humor about the antics of young children?*
5. *Does the parent seem patient and understanding with his or her own child?*
6. *When the child speaks to the parent does the parent truly listen and respond?*
7. *When discipline is necessary does the parent avoid the issue or deal directly with it? Does this involve screaming across the room or approaching the child and dealing with the situation face to face and with understanding?*
8. *Is a warm friendly greeting part of the parent's approach to your child in casual meetings?*

9. *How does the parent react to minor spills and accidents?*
10. *Do you feel comfortable talking with the parent? Have you some things in common (older siblings, interests, age, profession)?*

Often if you have met the parent at a Y class or another social place, you will have had the opportunity to have done some evaluation already and perhaps decided that the interactions you have witnessed fit into your mode of child rearing. But what if that is not the case? Do not despair. Our suggestion is that you set up as many informal meetings as you can with both the parent and child. Invite them to accompany you to the park or to come over to your home for a playtime. Let the children play while you chat. Believe us . . . with young children enough incidents will occur in a morning of play to observe and note the positive parent-child interactions you are looking for.

One of us avoided a disaster by a little vigilance and good sense. In the initial stage of a playgroup (three parents looking for a fourth) a neighbor was under consideration. One morning this person's child was playing at the neighbor's house. When the child came home he told his mother that he was made to sit in a chair for a certain period of time and not to move for some action he had done. While the parent realized all too well that her child was by no means an angel, she thought that the punishment was a little severe for a two-and-a-half-year-old child. She would have definitely preferred to have had him sent home. She decided to discuss the incident with the neighbor. After the discussion the parent whose child's behavior was in question decided that the punishment did not fit the crime, especially for a two-year-old, and that perhaps this neighbor's perception of normal two-year-old behavior was vastly different from her own. She decided as well that punishment of this sort did not fit her way of dealing with young children and perhaps it was best not to involve this person in the playgroup. Happily, a few weeks later a fourth member was found and the playgroup completed a successful year.

In our playgroup we decided we were definitely not interested in someone who could not handle some degree of mess in the house or on the children. Children are messy creatures—they enjoy dirt; they love mud pies; they are curious about how finger paint feels on their noses, arms, and shirts. Young children are also just beginning to become coordinated. Accidents will inevitably occur—juice will spill, "play dough" will fall down, perhaps during cooking time an entire bowl of batter will be knocked over. If a person cannot handle these occasional mishaps with a sense of humor, perhaps having young children in their charge isn't a good idea. Such flexibility may be hard to discover ahead of time, but some clues can be found after time spent together. What is the person's reaction to having juice spilled onto a new pair of pants? When you were together in the park and the children found the mud puddle before you did, what was the parent's reaction? Though perhaps different than yours could you accept it?

In essence we are suggesting that you observe and then evaluate parent-child interactions as much ahead of time as possible so you are in a position to make intelligent judgments about a proposed playgroup participant.

Bringing the Participants Together. So you've assembled four parents and children. The next step is to let the children meet and get well acquainted. There are a few ways of dealing with the settling-in process depending upon whether the children are familiar or unfamiliar with each other. For a group in which the participants have already spent time together we suggest you jump in with both feet, set up your schedule and off you go. If, however, you are a group that is unfamiliar with each other, let us give you a sample settling-in procedure. This type of gradual introduction to the playgroup routine might spare you the melodrama of a clutching child flooding you with tears as you try to inch your way out of the door. It usually takes an anxious child several relaxed visits to feel comfortable. No big deal, just invite everyone over on a nice day to play, snack, and have fun. It is best to do this at everyone's home so the children feel as if they have at least seen each setting before playgroup begins. Once that has been accomplished, set up a limited schedule for the first few sessions. For example: Sessions I and II meet only for an hour, sessions III and IV for an hour and a half. By session V the children have played together and have met and interacted with each participating parent without their own parent present. They have discovered that their parents have indeed returned after each playgroup session and are more likely to be comfortable and ready to begin the full playgroup program. You will find that the majority of the children will catch on quickly, and once they do you're ready to go.

PLAYGROUP GUIDELINES

Here is a summary of guidelines to make your playgroup successful from the start.

1. *The success of a playgroup depends upon the careful selection of the participants.*
2. *Before playgroup begins, have the children meet several times with the parents so that they can get acquainted.*
3. *Responsibility for running the playgroup rotates among the parents involved. On any given playgroup day one parent is in charge, allowing the remaining parents free time. The playgroup is held in the home of the parent in charge.*
4. *Four children is an ideal number for beginning social contacts and a reasonable number for parents to work with in a home setting.*
5. *It's best to have a homogeneous group (age span not varying more than six months), since children develop different*

skills at different ages. If you keep the age span close together, it will be easier for all to enjoy your projects, games, and activities.

6. *Days and time(s) of playgroup can be flexible. With certain groups, depending upon the age of the children and parental needs and desires, a morning playgroup may be lengthened to include lunch. In a playgroup that we are familiar with, as the children progressed through the year, they enjoyed making their own lunches and eating together.*

7. *Set up a flexible time schedule for activities, for example a two-hour playgroup can organize the time as follows:*
   9:30–10:00 Free play
   10:00–10:30 Special project
   10:30–11:00 Snack and story
   11:00–11:30 Outside play, music, and rhythm

8. *Be prepared. Make sure your projects are well thought out and your materials collected before the children arrive.*

9. *Make sure all parents involved understand that playgroup is not baby-sitting but rather a time for organized preschool activities.*

3

CREATING THE PHYSICAL ENVIRONMENT

DELECTABLE COLLECTIBLES

Now you have your parents and a few ground rules. Do you have the equipment you need? The following is a checklist of basic preschool equipment:

1. *Art Materials—tempera paint, paintbrushes, Play-Doh (you can be resourceful and make your own "play dough"; see Chapter 6), Magic Markers, crayons, paper of assorted sizes and colors, small bottles of glue, rounded scissors*
2. *Manipulative Materials—sewing cards, beads and string, pegboards, blocks and other small construction equipment, molding materials*
3. *Visual Discrimination Materials—shape sorters, color games, card games, lotto games, dominoes (pictures, shapes, numbers, colors)*
4. *Dramatic Play Materials—wooden or cardboard stand for store, house, or whatever; dress-up clothes, props (carriage, shopping cart, cash register), dolls*

5. *Musical Materials—records, record player, simple instruments*

6. *Language Materials—children's books, puppets, flannel board and flannel shapes*

7. *Furniture and Storage Space—small table and chairs, shelves for storing and displaying toys, bins for storing individual play materials*

8. *Outdoor Equipment—sandbox and sand toys, swings and climbing apparatus, riding toys*

People closely involved with preschool children, whether parents, teachers, or caregivers, are probably worth their weight not in gold but in "usable junk." Anybody working with children should be particularly tuned in to recyclable materials.

HOUSEHOLD ITEMS

First and foremost are the general, run-of-the-mill household items that can be saved for art and/or building projects. Below is a list of items commonly tossed in the trash by untrained eyes.

- *egg cartons*
- *milk cartons or jugs*
- *Styrofoam meat trays*
- *cardboard fruit trays*
- *orange juice cans*
- *toilet paper rolls*
- *paper towel rolls*
- *empty spice bottles*
- *colorful junk mail*
- *old greeting cards*
- *small boxes (matches, spices, Jell-O)*
- *bottle caps (plastic)*
- *yogurt containers and lids*
- *margarine containers and lids*

Many of these items are required for the art activities and projects we describe in the following chapters, so we'll mention here only a few possible uses of several items. For example, the cardboard and Styrofoam trays, as well as miscellaneous cardboard pieces, make excellent backing upon which to glue. You can make a funnel for sand or water play by cutting across a plastic milk jug below the handle, then inverting it. The lids from the yogurt and margarine containers can be used for stitchery, and the junk mail and greeting cards can be cut up for gluing or used as paper for simple cutting tasks. We often found that old greeting cards were exactly the right size and weight for the children to handle when they began to gain control of a pair of scissors. The best thing about these items, of course, is that they are free—you only need space to store them. You will soon notice, however, the rewards of your hoarding, since a collection of "usable junk," glue, and a child's imagination is usually all that is necessary for a creative and fun activity.

We know that storage of toys and supplies is always a problem. Proper storage assures maximum use of materials as well as encouraging children to establish good "clean-up-time" habits. The margarine or yogurt containers listed above are good for holding small items such as pegs or shape tiles or even art materials such as mixed paint or colored sand. With the lids in place, they become storage containers that can be safely used by children. And by using a pair of scissors and tape the gallon-size plastic milk jug can be turned into a low-cost storage space for toy people, furniture, cars, and trucks.

To make a storage container cut off the top of a large plastic bleach bottle and cover the edges with masking tape. Use on storage shelves for any small items.

RESOURCES FROM THE COMMUNITY

You'll want to approach merchants in the community for the next category of collectibles. We found people to be very receptive to our needs when they heard we wanted items for use with young children. Below is a list of useful items we found in our neighborhood.

Wallpaper Books. Any paint or home decorating store has books that are used by the customers to select wallpaper. However, when patterns of paper change and the companies issue new books, the store manager no longer needs the old books. Ask your local dealers to keep you in mind the next time a pattern change occurs. We are sure they will be most helpful. Once you have obtained a book or two, you will find they are excellent for cutting and pasting activities as well as discussions of color and texture.

Film Containers. The little, round containers in which rolls of 35-mm film are packaged can be acquired through a conversation with a salesperson in a photographic supply store. You can also ask any amateur photographer to save the containers for you. They are useful for gluing three-dimensional designs. Or how about filling them with rice, beans, or pebbles to make excellent shakers for a rhythm band or an "experiment in sound."

Wood Chips. Every lumber yard or carpentry shop has a scrap pile just taking up space. Usually you can find an excess of small interesting shapes that are of no use to the yard or shop, but that can be used by preschool children for gluing, coloring, and painting. Sometimes it is even possible to find larger scraps that, properly sanded, would enhance a block collection. Just ask!

Leather Scraps. Craftspeople who work in leather can often give you their scraps. They are frequently tossed aside, as they are too small to be of use, but these scraps provide an interesting added texture to a gluing project.

Clay. Local potters and small ceramic factories sometimes have excess clay that for one reason or another is not usable. Marilyn Ornstein once visited a stoneware factory in Tennessee and while watching a potter at work noticed a large bag of clay on the floor. Upon inquiring she was told it was the excess clay removed as the potter fashioned various plates and that it could not be used commercially. Thus that day Marilyn's playgroup acquired about 10 pounds of hardening clay!

Styrofoam Chips and Packing Pieces. There are several places where these items can be found, although securing them might require a little more scrounging on your part. Often stores receive equipment of one sort or another (medical, tools, audio) packed in large amounts of Styrofoam. It is all tossed out! The smaller Styrofoam "squiggles" can be used for stringing necklaces as well as gluing pictures. The larger Styrofoam pieces are often interesting shapes that lend themselves to building castle-like structures for small toy people, furniture, and cars. Just hand a few of these Styrofoam shapes to a group of children and watch what they become. They are certainly more inventive play pieces than store-bought castles or houses, and you can't beat the cost!

Large Refrigerator Cartons. If you have the space, excellent playhouses can be constructed from the cartons in which refrigerators are sold. Ask your local appliance store to save you one, or watch for new neighbors on your block! Windows and a door can be easily cut, curtains put on the windows, and you have a very inexpensive indoor playhouse. Hand the children paints or markers and let them decorate the house inside and out.

Other Large Cartons. The cartons in which other large items are delivered to stores can be also put to good use. Your local appliance dealer, supermarket, or department store usually has an abundant supply. With a little imagination and time, a carton of approximately 24 inches in height can be made into an excellent, sturdy play stove. You will need the following items:

regular packaging tape

black tape (cloth, plastic, or electrical)

5 small wooden knobs and matching screws

X-Acto knife

large piece of sturdy cardboard (preferably a side of another carton)

paint (optional)

To turn a carton into an ideal almost cost-free oven for your playgroup members:

1. *Select the side of the carton that you wish to be the top of the oven. Remember you want the carton to stand approximately 24 inches from the ground. The open side will either be on the floor or facing a side.*
2. *With black tape fashion burners on the top surface of the carton.*
3. *Attach each store-bought knob to the front side of the carton by making a small hole and inserting the knob and screw through the hole (as you would do on a wooden cabinet). In this way the knob can turn. If you wish to paint the knobs, do so before attaching them.*
4. *On the front side of the carton make three cuts to create an opening flap. Attach a knob to the center of the flap following the directions for knobs above. This is the oven door.*
5. *Using the large piece of cardboard, cut a shelf that can be inserted into the carton and secured with tape.*
6. *Turn the carton over, insert the shelf slightly below the opening. Secure with tape and then tape closed the open end of the carton.*
7. *Now, with the purchase of a few dishes and pots and pans, your preschoolers are ready to cook dinner for their parents: Don't forget that old plastic dishes and discarded pots and pans can be purchased very inexpensively at thrift shops or yard sales.*

Old Telephone Wire Spools. Telephone companies obtain new wiring on large and small wooden spools. They frequently have no further use for the spools and are happy to give them away if you are willing to cart them off yourself. These spools have many uses for outdoor activities. In Chapter 11 we have some suggestions and directions for turning these spools into inexpensive equipment.

Paper. Preschoolers love to draw and they can use a good amount of paper every session. The most economical way to provide the playgroup with as much paper as the children need is to track down used computer paper. Any office, factory, or place of business that uses a computer will surely have a supply of already run programs and data sheets that they no longer need. The paper is of good weight and size and can be used in individual sheets (cut on the perforated lines) or with several sheets together if the project calls for a large piece of paper. Our households have functioned on computer paper for years through the goodness of science departments at local universities. Anyone who has access to a computer will probably save you more than you need.

Fabric Scraps and Yarn. Many of the projects and art activities we discuss in the following chapters require yarn or fabric. Of course, these items can be purchased at any yard goods store in your neighborhood, but this is likely to be costly. And you can easily obtain yarn and fabric from friends and relatives who sew and knit. A simple request to them about saving useless fabric pieces and yarn scraps will yield you a year's supply of materials for any project we mention.

ENVIRONMENTAL RESOURCES

The last area of collectibles can be found in the great outdoors. Natural objects are not only fun for children to collect together, but of course are very useful for crafts as well as nature study.

If you are planning a trip to the shore (or know someone who is) take along an extra few bags for shells. A collection of any-sized shells can yield many craft activities. Large shells are fun to paint, and the smaller shells are good for gluing. Keep a supply of pinecones, interesting rocks, acorns, leaves in season, and even sticks throughout the year. Remember, young children love to glue and the more interesting supply of items you have, the more imaginative they will be!

We would like to close this chapter with an interesting concept that we have learned of recently. A recycling center that redistributes most of the materials we have just mentioned is presently operating in Greenfield, Massachusetts. The center operates for the community at large and is used primarily by the teachers of all grades and subjects in the area. However, non-teachers can also take any items they need and all residents are encouraged to support the center by contributing recyclable materials. If you have such a center in your community you are indeed lucky. If not, perhaps this will be an incentive to start one. It certainly is an invaluable resource to the people in the community who work with children, and it encourages children to "think ecology" as well.

4

CREATING THE SOCIAL ENVIRONMENT

A HAPPY PLACE TO VISIT

"The morning went smoothly," remarked Sheryl as we picked the children up after her first session with playgroup. But they never went near each other or spoke to each other most of the time. She added, "Did I do something wrong?" We assured her that was not the case. Our children were young two-year-olds when our playgroup began. Children of this age are really pre-social. They are just beginning to reach out to others, to communicate with others, and in fact to search out companionship. And this is what playgroup is all about—to help the children socially and to guide them in developing many kinds of skills.

THE BEGINNINGS OF COMMUNICATION: HELPING THE CHILDREN INTERACT

Preschoolers are complex little people. When they are faced with large groups of children, they become overwhelmed. Your home can be just the right type of protected social environment for them to open up and begin to grow. They learn to talk and play with big people and little tots like themselves. They're outside *their* home, yet inside *a* home, in a very special and very privileged club. They're naturally apprehensive at first. A little understanding and some gentle coaxing goes a long way. Glen had a difficult time leaving his mother and started the first few playgroup sessions in tears. We all keyed in on him and managed to make him more comfortable with us. Of course, some may say we overdid it; Glen went from crying when playgroup began to crying when it was over.

Your play area should be set up ahead of time with all toys and activities accessible. Prepare an activity that will attract the children's attention (for example, a water table filled with funnel cups, eyedroppers, and soapy bubbles). When they see it they'll leave their parents more easily. Join the fun. Meet the children at the door. Stoop down to their level. How about a warm smile? Let them know what you have planned. You'll be surprised how quickly they "settle in." When Jed heard what we had to offer, he gave us a big bear hug.

Early playgroup sessions will have you totally involved in the children's play. You'll be building with blocks, mixing the sand, helping to put together the puzzles. We sat with the children on the floor and became part of the group. If there were any problems, we were there to handle them quickly and quietly.

Security in the social environment sets off a whole slew of positive behavioral traits. Our kids became very affectionate with each other during playgroup and casual visits as well. There were scenes such as hugging each other upon arrival, holding hands while swinging, and concern for each other's distress.

Jed, who in the beginning tended not to reach out to other children though he happily played alone, was really helped by playgroup. The kids, without our instigation, made a concerted effort to include Jed in all their activities. They would not begin a circle game without taking Jed's hand. The more familiar he became with the other children, the more he wished to become part of the group. Was Ann pleasantly surprised to see Jed run up to Naomi in the supermarket shouting, "That's my playgroup friend."

Even seemingly negative social behavior such as pulling a toy away from another child is a beginning social behavior. The children are no longer isolated but are reacting to others in their environment. They will gradually learn to wait turns, share toys, and communicate desires verbally rather than physically. At this young age, the play that you will see is commonly called parallel play. That is, the children will play alone with the toys available while occupying the same physical space. They will ordinarily not initiate play with each other. However, with adult supervision or the adult as the cohesive force they will play in a group.

Don't be surprised if you find your personality clashes with that of one of the children. Preschoolers can have some very annoying traits. Over the years, we had to deal with the poky child who is always three steps behind the rest of the group, the overaggressive hyperactive child (there she is—bouncing off the wall), the excessively shy youngster (see him over there in the corner?), the whining tattletale, and lots more. Try to remember these few points and it will help. First, inherent in the concept of playgroups is the trust that children's parents place in you to seek out their youngsters' positive sides and gently guide them around their more negative traits. That's a responsibility you must be willing to accept. Second, one of the goals of a playgroup for preschoolers is to help them grow socially. By displaying any negative feelings you may have toward one of the children, you retard all members' growth. Now this does not mean that you should not maturely guide and point out wrongs where they occur. By all means, you should. But do it nicely, with a sense of humor, and restrain yourself from excessive lecturing or editorializing. Finally, there's a sense of accomplishment you will notice, as we did, when you realize you can guide a group of varied children, even if you're not in love with every one of them.

Kids love to be active, but sometimes one gets a bit physical. Don't overreact. Just remind the child that "we should use our mouths, not our hands." One of your jobs is to help solve any quarrels. If that doesn't do the trick, resort to removing the child from the situation for a "time-out" to cool all tempers. For us, physical punishment was definitely taboo. Rather, the last resort would be calling the parent. In three years with three separate groups this never happened, and we can assure you our children are normal, healthy kids.

Children have different interests and abilities and you might find all four children doing totally different activities and yet being totally content in the playgroup environment. If you have prepared an art activity for the group and no one shows an interest in it, don't be discouraged. We know you think the art project you've planned is terrific, but the kids aren't interested that day. What do you do? Don't force the children to do it. Next time playgroup meets at your house, pull it out again and who knows, it might be just the activity that one of the children wants to explore.

We decided the children didn't have to participate in any activity they didn't want to. As long as they were content, so were we. Over the year, even the shyest children progressed as long as we didn't turn them off by forcing projects.

Flexibility plays a big part in the success of your day. Note the mood of the kids as they arrive. Has it been raining for the last four days? Today is it finally sunny? Perhaps you ought to spend time outdoors first. After some good fresh air and exercise, they might be more apt to do quiet activities. As with any other job you undertake you are going to experience good and bad days. Some days the children will have fewer sharing problems, some days more need for running and physical play. Roll with them. Don't be afraid to chuck a whole day's plan if you

think the group could profitably spend two hours outside. Use your instincts; if things are not running smoothly, take them out for a walk, or find another activity to break the routine.

Don't be surprised if after two hours you find very tired children on your hands, waiting patiently or not so patiently for a parent to come. Two hours of sustained interactions, conflicts, and mental and physical activity are exhausting for preschoolers, and for you too. This social business is their work, and work is tiring. Remember also that children cope differently with fatigue. One might withdraw with a thumb stuck firmly in mouth, while another might become more "hyper" with every passing minute. This might be a time for you to gently sing, do a finger play, or turn on a calm record. Some children, yours included, may simply fall apart at pick-up time. Jed was our screamer at this time. Ann would arrive and Jed would be screaming he didn't want to go home. In reality, he didn't. On the other hand, he needed to. His crying and screaming were his way of releasing the tensions of an intense morning for a two-year-old. We understood, although it was unnerving to watch. We were so happy that Ann was not a ninety-pound, fragile woman; she would never have gotten Jed to the car.

LEARNING TO SHARE: A BASIC SOCIAL SKILL

Sharing. That's rough for children. It's bad enough that they have to share their toys, but they have to share you too. You can expect to spend a good deal of your time in the beginning of playgroup dealing with the "sharing problem." The emergence of a desire to be social means just that. Children need to learn how. Learning to share is the first big step toward that end. They have to learn sometime, and there's no better place for children to begin to learn to work and play with others than in a playgroup. It really prepares them for the organized schools ahead. Letting the host child have a few special jobs really helps. Ours passed out the snack and chose the book for story time. Mitch required Tricia's hand while playing and her lap while reading, and he got it. This extra show of concern checked his anxiety and resolved the problem.

Pulling toys away from others is common behavior for young preschoolers. Don't be shocked to see your mild-mannered children become aggressive when the need to share their toys arises. For a preschooler, "That's mine" is a phrase used more often than not. If a toy does not lend itself to group play, we limited the time each child could play with it. Using a kitchen timer was very helpful. It was a sight-and-sound reminder that released us from being the "ogre." We set it for a limited time (five minutes) and then reminded the child that when the bell rang, it was time to pass the toy to the next child.

We suggest that you be firm about it, even if the reaction is a flood of tears. The children will become accustomed to the rules after a while. Children need to learn rules and limits provided, of course, that they are reasonable and understandable. Learn the children's reactions to giving up a toy. One may be comforted by a hug, another by a diversion. Maybe one needs to have the next toy on hand right as the buzzer rings. You'll soon learn how best to cope with each one. Above all be consistent! Children profit from consistent adult behavior; it will help them conform to the rules more quickly and easily.

Certain group toys such as blocks may require you to become directly involved to preserve the peace. Sit down on the floor with the children and help them see how everyone can be involved in the play. Show them how to build an airport. Talk about the things you will need. Have one child build the control tower, others the terminal and runways. When things are running smoothly, you can assume a back seat in the activity and let the children initiate further play. If a child has already built a structure and doesn't want anyone to add to it, grant the request provided that the child has not monopolized all the blocks.

Another sharing problem can arise when a special toy has been brought from home to be shown but not touched by other children. Cries of protest from the other children rapidly follow. We dealt with this situation by gathering the playgroup into a circle and letting the child display the treasure to all. When everyone had had a turn to see it, we put it away for safekeeping.

COMMUNICATION AMONG PARENTS

During your preplaygroup visits, take the opportunity to touch on sticky subjects like discipline and philosophy. After a bit of generalizing, we naturally entertained some specific problems. What to do if your child won't let you leave? What about the overphysical child?

What do you do with the preschooler who is being toilet trained? This became a serious disturbance to one of our parents who eventually opened up and discussed with the group her resentment at having to continually change another child's dirty diaper. Our decision: Parents should not have to interrupt milestones in their children's development because of playgroup. In many ways, you will be asked to act as surrogate parent during these few hours per month. This requires a sense of maturity and sacrifice. But more importantly, it points out one of the subtle elements of a successful playgroup—parent communication. Whenever a problem surfaced with any of the children we discussed it. Changing diapers, for instance, was a real problem in one parent's mind until it was brought out in the open. Once she exposed her resentment, it became quite manageable. She didn't like to do it but could accept it. We learned to respect each other and look for dialogue. It occurred almost daily, and we were surprised to find that others see qualities in our children that we had overlooked, forgotten, or found maybe a little difficult to deal with. Tricia and Mitchell in our own playgroup had personalities as opposite as two sides of a coin. While Tricia moved quickly and impulsively through the day's events and activities, Mitchell was a slow-moving, observant, and deliberate individual. Inevitable clashes between two very different personalities occurred. Whereas Tricia realized the very positive aspects of this type of personality, dealing with it on a day-to-day basis caused some conflicts. We in the playgroup responded to these personality traits in a very positive fashion, even capitalizing on them. Taking walks with Mitchell his way was a wonderful experience. He took the time to observe his surroundings to the fullest, finding the most interesting leaves, letter-shaped twigs, bugs of various sizes and shapes, and other sundry items in nature. We had to give him the award for the most interesting collections on our walks—even though sometimes we never made it to our destination!

During our interviewing we asked parents about the communication problem. They were very honest with us and pointed out some possible problems. One group of parents interviewed felt that they did not know each other well enough to be truly open and honest with each other. A teacher from Chapel Hill, North Carolina, wrote in response to our question "Was the communication between parents adequate?"—"No, at times group members sensed a problem with a child, but were too uncomfortable to tackle it directly. Parents of children this young confuse a problem a child is having with assuming it is a negative reflection on the parent. We all needed to ease up and talk more freely and specifically." Another parent, from Chapel Hill, North

Carolina, commented, "In retrospect, I think it would have been helpful if we had gotten together for lunch to compare notes and exchange ideas and feelings periodically." From these comments and our own observations we learned that talking around the issues does not rectify situations or problems and that no growth will take place unless the participants keep the channels of communication open.

One of the fringe benefits of playgroups for the parents is a chance to discuss and understand childhood behavior. It's amazing how in almost every case, that distressing trait you associated with your child alone in all the world turns out to be quite age typical. How reassuring it can be to see someone else's child covered with dirt and a morning snack or responding to a challenge with brute violence. It helps you realize that your kids are not so unusual after all.

What happens if you get sick on your playgroup day? One of the amazing things about our three-year experience is that not once was a scheduled meeting cancelled because of illness. If parents were sick, they called and arranged to switch days with another parent. This not only prevented our children, who looked forward to their meetings, from being disappointed, but also gave the sick parent a few hours' rest.

As far as childhood illnesses went, we made a general rule. If a child was running a fever or had a communicable disease (such as chicken pox or strep throat), we kept them home. This spared us some of the rapid-fire group illnesses often seen in day-care centers with large numbers of children under one roof. We did not keep children home for runny-nose, viral illness. They looked forward to coming and realistically we felt that occasionally catching a bug was something to be expected with any gathering of children.

Whenever a group of children gets together there is always a possibility that injuries may occur. Though ours were never serious and confined to bumps and bruises, it is a wise idea for each parent to provide the telephone numbers of parent's workplace and the child's pediatrician. With adequate supervision, we never experienced a serious injury with five separate playgroups. Yet the knowledge that you are prepared for such an occurrence will make you more secure.

Problems are bound to come up even in the most ideal situation. But when dealing with preschoolers, remain flexible and alter the situation to fit the needs of the children. You'll be pleasantly surprised, as we were, at how much you have to offer. No baby-sitter will be able to give the love and understanding to your preschooler that you, the parent, can. Be confident. Take the plunge.

5

COMMUNICATION

LET'S PRETEND

OK, let's do some things that will increase verbal skills. You say your preschoolers are too verbal as it is? No. You just think they are. We're talking about drama, imagination, and fun. Our play equipment consisted of many types of old clothes for dress up and accessories such as an old doctor's bag, jewelry, and an old trunk that could easily be converted into anything imaginable. One family had constructed a wooden frame that alternately became a store, a post office, or any other building desired. Dishes, any type of play sink or stove, and a small table with chairs help provide an atmosphere just perfect for a "coffee break." With a little encouragement from a parent, kids can be drawn into conversations about what they're cooking and serving.

Get involved! Use all your resources—props, music, and costumes. Before playgroup begins one morning, line up several chairs in the play area. Leave pocketbooks with play money, pieces of paper for tickets, and various hats. When the children arrive, put a train record on the phonograph and before you know it they'll be on an imaginary train ride. During this time you can use words such as engineer, conductor, ticket, whistle, and locomotive. The children will soon be using these words along their "ride." Let each child experiment with a different role. After setting up the right atmosphere for this type of play, you can't help but notice the enormous amount of communication that is generated.

Here are a few more "stages" you can set for encouraging dramatic play. While reading the suggestions take note of the enormous amount of language learning that will naturally accompany this type of play situation.

Zoo Trip

MATERIALS:

chairs/zoo animal pictures (elephant, monkey, seal, bear, giraffe)

Line up several chairs for a bus ride to the zoo. Place the various pictures of the zoo animals in different parts of the room. You be the "tour guide" and direct the bus to each "cage area." Once there, have the children become the animals they are visiting by moving like those animals. For example, swinging their arms like the elephant's trunk or eating bananas like monkeys. Visit all the animals, and then climb back on the bus for the ride back home.

Fire! Fire!

MATERIALS:

chairs/inner cardboard tube from wrapping paper rolls/fire hats (purchased or homemade)/bell

What small child doesn't like to dramatize fire fighters riding in the fire truck! Have several chairs set up for the truck and don't forget the seat at the rear! Provide each child with a hat and a cardboard tube for a hose and bring out the bell. Clang the bell, climb aboard, and the children will no doubt do the rest.

Supermarket

MATERIALS:

empty shelf or tabletop/empty cans of soup or vegetables, empty boxes of foodstuffs, margarine tubs/play money/

purses, wallets/play cash register (store-bought or suitably decorated shoe box)

Set out the empty foodstuff containers on the shelf or table. Using the play money, wallets, and purses take a trip to the grocery store to buy food for supper. Let someone be the cashier and collect the money for the cash register from the shoppers. A good deal of practical language will be used in this dramatic play, and it might even lead the children into trying new types of food.

Is There a Doctor in the House?

MATERIALS:

chairs/dolls/tongue depressors/Popsicle sticks/cotton balls/ old, white men's shirts/egg carton/string/used hypodermic syringes available from your pediatrician

Line up the dolls in the room. Bring out all the materials above, and you are ready for office hours. Thermometers can be made out of the Popsicle sticks and a play stethoscope can be rigged up by stringing a single section from an egg carton onto a long string. Tongue depressors, cotton balls, and used syringes will add to the realism of this dramatic play. This activity can be really beneficial for young children as many of them do experience some anxiety when visiting the doctor. Don't be surprised if you find yourself the children's next patient! Play along, and let them fix you up.

Barber Shop

MATERIALS:

white apron/tissues/plastic safety razor/soft brush/soap and water/picture of hair/cash register/table/chair

This activity is a bit messy, so old clothes and easy wipe up space is advisable. You might want to set this activity up outside in warm weather. How refreshing it will be to have cool water patted on your face! The children will have such fun mixing the soap and water to form foamy beards and mustaches!

Bakery

MATERIALS:

cookie sheet/cookie cutters/eggbeaters/"play dough"/measuring cups/spoons/cash register/table/chairs

What will we have for snack today? How about an imaginary trip to the bakery? There is a part for everyone to play, bakers, salesperson, customers. Set out all the baking utensils and the "play dough" for the work area. Next set aside an area with cash register for displaying the finished baked goods. After a full morning of rolling, kneading, and twisting the dough, a "real" treat is in order for such hard workers.

Post Office

MATERIALS:

index cards/ink pads/rubber stamps/used envelopes/stamps, i.e., Easter seals/crayons, pencils/boxes with slits

Set up a table with ink pads, rubber stamps, and adhesive stamps. Alongside this have boxes with slits in the top to be used as mailboxes. On the side you might write out-of-town mail, in-town mail. On the other side of the room have a table with envelopes, index cards, pencils, and crayons on it. The children can write letters or draw pictures for their parents or relatives, and then it's off to the post office to mail them.

Party Time

MATERIALS:

set of plastic cups/saucers and dishes/small plastic pitcher/ paper napkins/dry cereal such as Cheerios/party hats

Any time can be party time. Put on some old party hats to set the mood. The children can take turns pouring and serving the treats.

6

MANIPULATION AND COORDINATION

LITTLE FINGERS BUSY AT WORK

Preschoolers are beginning to get it all together physically. So why not work a bit on manipulative skills. That's just a way of describing activities that build and strengthen small hand muscles and at the same time help coordination of the hands and eyes. For example, the task of stringing beads requires a child to grasp steadily a string and thread it through beads of various sizes. Building with blocks, molding "play dough," stringing beads, sewing, cutting with scissors, using crayons, painting with brushes, and using Magic Markers are some of the things that give children the opportunity to practice eye-hand coordination while strengthening and controlling small muscles. In our group we set out a few of these activities every time we met. We varied the materials according to the children's interests. Jed loved to cut, Naomi enjoyed drawing, and "play dough" appealed to all. These skills are prerequisites for the development of dexterity needed for writing, tying, and dressing. Let us give you an example. If you could observe the young preschooler holding a large crayon or pencil, you would note several things. The child's

grasp would be awkward. The pencil would be somewhat shaky in the child's hand. The writing would be random, and at times the marks would be too light to be seen on the paper. The child would perhaps not be able to exert enough pressure on the pencil or crayon to create visible marks. Over the next few years the child's ability to write will increase. The awkwardness of grasping will be gone, and the child will be able to control the pencil's movement. The strokes will appear strong and controlled. As time goes on, with practice in holding and working with pencils and crayons, as well as practice in other eye-hand coordination activities, the child will be able to write in confined spaces and reproduce shapes and letters on lines in the proper order. These changes are related to the exercise and strengthening of the child's muscles through use. The child is now ready to print letters of the alphabet, numbers, and words and to tie shoes, zip zippers, and do other similar tasks. The child has mastered control of hands for future academic and social use. Here are some specific suggestions for manipulative activities.

Cutting

MATERIALS:

rounded scissors/pieces of construction paper or any semi-thick paper

Cutting sounds easy, but it's not. It takes quite a lot of practice and patience on your part. Some of your preschoolers may not be able to master it at first. Start by giving the children a piece of paper and teach them to fringe the edges by opening and closing the scissors all along the paper border. Once they've got that, try cutting up one-inch strips of paper. With some mastery of the skill, they will be able to cut off small pieces from the strip. Meet the success with thunderous applause. They deserve it. We still smile when we remember Glen's mother commenting, "You know what I like about motherhood? I cut paper dolls so well now."

"Play Dough"

INGREDIENTS:

1 C flour/½ C salt/1 C water/1 T vegetable oil/2 t cream of tartar/choice of food coloring

Mix all ingredients together in a heavy saucepan. Cook until mixture forms a ball. Store in plastic wrap or coffee cans in the refrigerator.

OTHER MATERIALS:
rollers/blunt pencils/toothpicks/cookie cutters/dull knives/ mallets

This recipe is a whiz. It makes the very best nonstick, nonmess "play dough," and the kids love it. There's no end to what you can do with it. There are endless varieties of activities and uses for play dough. After they squish it, squash it, mush it, and mash it to their hearts' content, bring out the utensils. Take out the toothpicks, blunt pencils for poking, cookie cutters for making shapes, mallets for pounding, and dull knives for cutting. The texture is beautiful and the moldability amazing. With a little imagination, you can easily "wow" the kids. Take, for instance, the day Ann set aside a kitchen cabinet to "bake" the children's play dough cookies and cakes. When they returned to see if the cookies were baked, they were flabbergasted. Their cookies had been magically transformed into real treats. This game was repeated over and over again to the children's delight.

Baker's Clay—Bread Dough Art

INGREDIENTS:
1½ C warm water/1 C salt/4 C flour

Mix the water and the salt together and then add the flour. Knead for fifteen minutes. Wrap in plastic wrap if you do not plan on using it right away.

OTHER MATERIALS:
Tempera paint/shellac/paintbrushes

Here's a good one, an activity that's instant fun and lasts long enough to show Mom and Dad. Kids can even hang their work in their rooms. Just roll out dough with the children. Give them each a handful and let them create any shape desired, from hands to hanging wall decorations. After the shape is made put foil on a cookie sheet and bake the shapes at 275° for three hours. At your next meeting you can pick up where you left off by painting or shellacing the works of art. You don't have to be an artist to have fun here. Remember the seasonal possibilities. Since Naomi's birthday was on Halloween, the playgroup baked her "clay pumpkins" to hang for Halloween decorations. Use your cookie cutters and create Christmas trees and gingerbread people. And by all means don't forget hearts with "I love you" on Valentine's Day.

Stringing

MATERIALS:

yarn/glue/rigatoni noodles/chariot wheel noodles/cut straws/ other paper shapes with holes/other tubular objects

You don't have to go hunting in stores for stringing supplies. They're all over the house. Anything with a hole will do. The night before playgroup, dip a bunch of pieces of yarn in glue and let them harden. The next morning, put your objects in individual pans and let your kids choose. What's your job? Help little hands that fumble and talk about the colors and shapes. Be sure to tie a knot around one noodle at the end so objects don't slip and tears don't flow. Imagine Thanksgiving with these homemade Indian bead necklaces.

Sewing

MATERIALS:

yarn/blunt needles/plastic lids from coffee cans, margarine tubs, other containers/paper/Styrofoam meat trays

Sewing preschooler style takes a little special preparation. Punch large obvious holes in plastic lids, paper, or Styrofoam plates. Secure yarn in large blunt needles. For extra fun, let the kids pick their favorite color yarn. Help them go in and out of the holes making any design they like. If you want to be really neat, glue their work between two suitable pieces of construction paper. Voila! A masterpiece is framed.

Coloring

MATERIALS:

paper/Magic Markers/crayons

So what's so new and exciting about coloring? It's been around a long time. Well, try a new twist. Lay out some large blocks of different shapes or large cookie cutters and let your children trace the shapes they wish to color. Large 3-foot coloring books available in many supermarkets and department stores are quite inexpensive and offer children the chance to color something their own size. Or if you want something exactly their size, take a trip to your local newspaper and purchase a roll of old newsprint paper. Lie the children down on a long sheet and trace them with a Magic Marker, then let them color themselves. Now that you're in the spirit, let your imagination fly, and think of some new twists on coloring yourself.

Rings and Hooks

MATERIALS:

1 wooden board approximately 12 by 12 inches/12 cup hooks of varying sizes/12 metal washers of varying sizes/ small box

Screw the cup hooks onto the board, making three rows with four hooks on each. Place the washers in the small box. Have the children hang the washers on the hooks in any way they wish. Later on in the year, as they become more familiar with the board, you can begin to work on size discrimination with the children matching large washers with large hooks and smaller washers with small hooks.

Geo-Boards

MATERIALS:

small wooden boards, approximately 4 by 4 inches/nails about one inch in length with small heads/colored rubber bands (large sizes that are easy to stretch)

Make a board for each child by hammering one nail into each corner. When the boards are completed the children are ready to learn how to stretch the rubber bands from one nail to another, creating any patterns that they wish. In the beginning, when these boards are first introduced, you may need to help the children by holding one side of the rubber band around a nail while they stretch it to another nail. You'll be surprised at how quickly they will catch on and the pleasing patterns that will emerge!

Beans in a Can

MATERIALS:

small orange juice cans with lids (enough for each child to have one)/masking tape/various types of beans (examples: lima, kidney, black-eyed peas, split peas)/small Styrofoam trays (one for each child)

Here is an activity designed to give preschoolers practice in using their small hand muscles by picking up beans of various sizes. Make a hole in each lid large enough to accommodate the largest bean. Seal the lid on each orange juice can with tape. Place a small number of beans on a Styrofoam tray for each child to use. Have the children pick up the beans and insert them into the cans one or two at a time. Begin with the larger-size beans (lima and kidney) and progress to the smaller kinds later (black-eyed peas and split peas). Remember that dry beans are slippery and can be quite a challenge for little fingers!

Nuts and Bolts

MATERIALS:

varying sizes of nuts and bolts found at any hardware store/ shoe box

Place the nuts and bolts in a box and let the children explore the various sizes. They will soon learn the pairs that go together and have fun assembling the pairs. Little fingers will get a great deal of practice turning the nuts and their muscles will certainly grow stronger.

Water Play Fun

MATERIALS:

tub filled with a small amount of water/plastic cloth/towels/squeeze toys such as poultry basters, eyedroppers, nasal syringes, sponges

For a two-year-old there is nothing more relaxing than water play. It also provides excellent practice in exercising little hands. Set out the tub on the plastic cloth on the floor or the table.

Keep a few towels handy for emergency spills. Fill the tub about one-third full of water. Give all the children squeezing toys and let them enjoy filling and emptying the implements. At another time you can give the children small plastic cups or containers and let them experiment with how long it takes to fill the cup using only a squeezing toy!

Paper Crunch

MATERIALS:
old newspapers/large paper sacks

With winters what they are in many portions of the country and fuel costs always on the rise, families are using fireplaces more and more. Here is an activity to make your playgroup members into fuel-conscious kids. Provide the children with cut-up sheets (one-half-page size) of newspaper. Have them use their hand muscles to "scrunch up" the newspaper as tightly as they can to make "fire starter" balls. Collect them in large paper sacks to be taken home at the end of the session. By the way, there are many times that you will be able to use paper balls in a craft activity. Always encourage the children to do the scrunching themselves!

Button Up, Zip Up

MATERIALS:
old clothing, such as jackets with buttons or zippers

There is probably not a better manipulative skill to begin to learn at this age than the ability to button and zip one's own clothing. Practicing on the real item is a good place to start. We found clothing at the local thrift shop. Make sure that the article of clothing has large enough buttons and is sturdy enough to manipulate. For example, a small child's jacket will work better than a floppy sweater. Make sure the item of clothing does not have too many buttons, which could be too frustrating for a young preschooler. When selecting an item with a zipper, make sure that the zipper is average size. Since the object at this time is to gain the ability to move the zipper up and down only, stitch the zipper together at the bottom so that it does not separate. In the beginning you might want to attach a small ring in the zipper end so that the children can more easily grasp it. If you are ambitious you can make a stiff cardboard figure or two that can be dressed in the articles of clothing so that the children can practice on the dolls. Now don't forget to let them work on their own coats at "going home time"!

7

CREATIVITY AND EXPLORATION OF MATERIALS

THE YOUNG PICASSOS

The art activities that we've just described were mainly for developing manipulative skills. But what about exploring different art media and encouraging creativity? Stay simple with your choice of activities. Remember preschoolers are short on concentration and coordination, so that even the seemingly simple task of gluing objects on a piece of paper is quite a feat. First, you demonstrate. Then let the children really use the media you have chosen. Each child's interests and capabilities will vary. Some children will explore the activity longer than others. Don't insist that children finish an art activity to your liking. Let them go as far as they like, and compliment their efforts. Don't teach the children here. Let them teach themselves. Try some of these activities, but keep a close eye on the children. Artistically creative children invariably wander to the clean wall or fine furniture.

GLUING

Gluing Crumbled Tissue

MATERIALS:

colored tissue paper/small bottles of white glue/cardboard

What a mess! You've got to be kidding! No, we're not. Actually white glue is water soluble and quite manageable. The kids love it. There's something about making an object stick that turns them on. Precut tissue paper into 2-inch random shapes. Place various colored shapes in a box. Have the children squeeze glue onto cardboard. Then have them crumble a tissue paper and place it on a glob of glue. When many tissue shapes have been glued, the result will be a collage. You can also precut cardboard shapes and make flowers, hearts, trees, or other figures.

Hard and Soft Gluing

MATERIALS:

hard objects—wood chips, bottle caps, yogurt tops, cardboard, linoleum pieces/soft objects—fabric, tissue paper, cotton balls, yarn/small bottles of white glue/Styrofoam meat trays/large pieces of cardboard

For all you "junk art" enthusiasts we have hard and soft gluing. Put a box of hard objects and a box of soft objects on the table. Discuss with the kids why each of the groups belongs together and the individual properties of the objects. Have the children place globs of glue on your meat trays or cardboard and let them choose objects to paste.

Fabric Gluing

MATERIALS:

different-textured fabrics—velvet, corduroy, wool, fur/glue/cardboard

Dig into that old sewing bag and pull out a batch of your most colorful materials. Precut fabric into different sizes and shapes. Then have the children place a glob of glue on the cardboard and paste. Try to find a variety of fabrics that will demonstrate obvious differences in textures. You might even set up a display of nonfabric objects (for instance, moss, a peach, a rose petal, pine bark, pinecones) that are natural examples of texture. Show them how the soft piece of velvet might be paired with the rose petal and so on down the line. Try cutting cardboard dolls and letting the kids dress them. You might ask the parents to dress the kids in solid basic colors that day and then help them make miniatures of themselves to bring home. See, touch, feel, and paste—key words here.

Paper Gluing

MATERIALS:

old cards/magazines/junk mail/catalogs/corrugated paper/ tinfoil/wax paper/colored construction paper

Paper gluing is good for design and shape. Have a large box filled with cut paper. Have the children place glue on construction paper and glue down cut pieces. This brings printed objects, figures, colors, and shapes into play and often leads to a visual poem. We remember the time Naomi cut a picture of a happy sun and said to Marilyn, "Here's a warm smile for you, Mommy!" There's a poetic side to preschoolers just begging to come out. If you think of it this way, it's a lot more fun. You can precut pictures of interest or take old magazines and catalogs and let them start from scratch.

Environmental Gluing

MATERIALS:

leaves/dandelions/rocks/cardboard/paper bags/acorns/pinecones/sticks

Kids, like adults, often take nature for granted. We all need to be reminded we're part of the world around us. So take a walk with a bag supplied to each child, and see what you can find. It doesn't matter whether you're in the country, suburbs, or city. Somehow objects are always plentiful, and often the most unlikely object stimulates a spontaneous story. We remember the time Mitchell picked up an old cigarette butt as one of his environmental gems. Rather than ordering him to discard it, Tricia saved it in her own bag until they reached home. She then peeled the paper from the old tobacco and explained how the paper was made from trees and the tobacco from special leaves. She explained how smoke from cigarettes and smoke from factories can dirty the air we breathe and read *Barbapapa's Ark* by Annette Tison and Talus Taylor (see Chapter 9, Stories) to put the idea of pollution in a story form. So you see that with a little imagination, the good and not-so-good "environmental treasures" that are brought home for pasting on cardboard can be fauna for the inquiring preschooler's mind.

Sand Gluing

MATERIALS:
dry tempera/sand/baby food jars with holes punched in the lids/old salt shakers/old spice jars/glue/cardboard

Sand gluing can be messy for preschoolers, so you might want to save this for outdoors on a nice warm spring day. It's a fun activity though, and kids just love the feel of sand, especially when it's full of color. Just mix dry tempera paint in sand. Pour the mixture into shakers. Give the children glue bottles and have them make a glue design on the cardboard. Then, while the glue is still wet, have them shake colored sand onto the glue pattern. Shake off excess sand and let the project dry thoroughly. Now we don't want to give away all our gems at once, but try this if you want to see some smiling faces. Use brown construction paper to cut out cones, and let the children pick their "flavor" ice cream from your colored construction paper. Cut out a double scoop and staple to the cone. Have them place glue on the "ice cream," and here comes the fun part. Take whatever color sprinkles you want, kids, and make that cone especially delicious.

Wallpaper Gluing

MATERIALS:
old wallpaper/glue/cardboard

Before you get too involved with gluing the precut shapes of differing color, design, and texture, give your youngsters a little information about why wallpaper is there at all. Here's a chance to say a few words on individual tastes and artistic preference. A stained board, painted board, and papered board are useful props to demonstrate some choices. Your own wall coverings help too. Now let them choose their favorite. And don't be surprised if they are able to tell you why they like it best. You'll probably be amazed to find, as we were, that these little minds have a primitive, yet very basic and true grasp of what they like in color, texture, and design.

3-D Gluing

MATERIALS:
heavy cardboard/paper towel rolls/wood chips/film containers/milk bottle tops/any other small items

We all know kids like to build. Well, here's a chance to let them go hog-wild with some freelance construction. Assemble items on the table. Let the children choose what they wish to glue. Encourage them to build up rather than build out. It's fun to ask them individually what they're building. You may need to give them a hand to help things stick properly. But beware not to infringe on their creative zeal by suggesting the next move. They don't want to have to share the credit with anyone. Once they've completed their "masterpieces" why not place them strategically on the floor and with the aid of cars and trucks guide them into dramatic play?

PAINTING

Finger Painting

MATERIALS:

Ivory Flakes/water/food coloring/vinyl wallpaper, shelving paper, freezer paper, cookie sheets

Put equal parts of Ivory Flakes and water in a mixing bowl. Let the children use a hand eggbeater to beat until the soapsuds are thick and fluffy.

To watch a child finger paint is to see an artist in motion, give or take a few sporadic excursions into noncanvas land. You'll see bold strokes, delicate spreading, dramatic gestures, and, yes, finishing applied with surprising skill. Just put a heaping tablespoon of finger paint on a smooth shiny surface (vinyl wallpaper, shelving paper, freezer paper, cookie sheets, or formica counters). If the children are finger painting on shelving paper or freezer paper, let the design simply dry. If they are using the other surfaces, when the design is completed take any piece of paper and lay it on top of the painting to make a print. A word to the wise: Keep a close eye on the Picassos. When set free, Mitchell decided that by using his arms, elbows, and feet he could definitely be more creative. If you want to amaze them, get involved! Show them how to thumbprint. Dip your thumb in the paint and press it on a piece of paper. Then take a pen or pencil and add some lines to the "body." And look! A frog, an owl, a puppy dog, or whatever.

Tempera

MATERIALS:

½ C dry tempera/1 C of dry detergent/water/½ t alum/ paintbrushes/any paper/muffin tins or other shallow containers

Why is it kids so love to get a brush in their hands? The large brushes work best. Mix all ingredients to desired consistency. Place paper on an easel or any flat surface. Put a little paint in shallow containers and provide the children with paintbrushes. Allow the children to create at will. With these tempera paints you needn't fear ingestion, self-artistry (paint from head to toe), or spills. Temperas are nontoxic and clean up simply with water. It is prudent to cover or remove any valuable fabrics, furniture, or rugs. For added fun, construct some makeshift easels indoors or out and let the children truly feel the glory of the artistic stroke. Only place a small amount of paint in shallow containers.

Sponge Painting

MATERIALS:

sponges cut into small pieces/clothespins/shallow pans/tempera paint/paper

This is a fun one. Cut pieces of sponge and attach them to clothespins. Pour a small amount of paint into shallow pans, no deeper than 1/16 of an inch or just enough to cover the bottom.

Wet the sponges and then have the children dip the sponges into the paint. Now let them hop along the paper and see what happens. Maybe now's the time to compare the "textured" print with a simple smooth stroke.

Block Printing

MATERIALS:

old blocks/spools/clothespin tops/wood pieces/cut oranges, potatoes, cucumbers/corks/shallow pans/newsprint or other paper/tempera paint

Here's a chance again to mix living and inanimate objects in a creative way. Wood blocks, spools, clothespins, and corks each have a shape and design you can copy with ink. Surprise! So do cut vegetables and fruits of all kinds. In fact, it's hard to improve on nature's beauty. Try placing a very small amount of paint in a shallow pan. Have the children dip the object in the paint and then print the paper. Unused newsprint from your local newspaper is best for this. We let the children make enough wrapping paper for their families' holiday gifts. As an added attraction, see if your local newspaper will loan you a few "type letters" or better yet, a picture plate. Take a newspaper and place it next to fresh newsprint. Dip the letters or picture in fresh ink and show the children how printing is done. It really drives home the point about imprint painting.

Texture Painting

MATERIALS:

sand/heavy cardboard/deep dishes for mixture/liquid tempera/thick brushes

Here's another lesson in texture not unlike sand gluing, but you have more freedom with this medium. Of course anywhere sand, paint, and children are combined, accidents do occur. So keep a watchful eye. Mix liquid tempera with sand until you have a thick consistency. Have the children brush the mixture onto heavy cardboard. Let the painting dry thoroughly.

Eyedropper Painting

MATERIALS:

eye or nose droppers/paper toweling/food coloring/muffin tins/water

Here's an art form that is pleasing to the eye and demonstrates spatial form. Mix water with several different food colors. Put small amounts into the muffin tins. Show the children how to squeeze the rubber tops of droppers to draw up the colored water and then to release the top over the paper towel. See how the colors spread to make a design. Why do you suppose they do that? Well, maybe you can help show them why if you've purchased a big old sea sponge at the supermarket the night before. Take a pan and fill it with enough water to approximately equal the capacity of your sponge. (Test the night before.) Add food coloring. Then proceed with your magical trick. Make the water disappear! Where did it go? Right inside the sponge because it has spaces for the water to hide inside. See the spaces? Now this sheet of paper towel has spaces too. They are very small and you can't see them unless you color your water and watch it spread from little hole to little hole. Everything is made of little parts with spaces in between, even things that look solid like you and me. And we can prove it, kids! Because when you get sweaty, hot water comes out on your skin. Where from? From your little spaces. You can see that art and science need not be worlds apart.

Watercolor Painting

MATERIALS:

small brushes/watercolor sets/water in a shallow pan or dish/paper toweling

Watercolor painting is a nice medium for children. It's not too messy, and the mixing and matching of colors that naturally occurs can make these childhood creations a delight. But there are pitfalls. Start by placing a piece of paper toweling at each child's place. This will be used as a blotter after they have rinsed their brushes to change colors. Show them how to dip their brushes into the water and then into the color they choose. After they are finished with one color, have the children dip their brushes into the clean water and blot out the excess paint. Ideally, colors will not mix, but if you notice that all the paints are turning a grayish brown, be patient! Perhaps it is time to re-teach the procedure. If all turns out well, you'll have a melding of form and color combinations. You may wish to follow this up at your next meeting with more experimentation with color combinations. Dixie cups with mixtures of color are helpful. And how about a plaid fabric that shows that when blue thread crosses red thread, it looks purple. Getting a feel for this? Good. Then be sure to have *The Ant and the Bee and the Rainbow* by Angela Banner (see Chapter 9, Stories) on hand. Here's a color book your kids will love.

Mural Painting

MATERIALS:

large sheet of newsprint/liquid tempera/brushes/muffin tin

What better way to teach cooperation than with a large mural painting? A few hints for success here. Save this project until the time when the group is all thoroughly acquainted and have a more positive than negative approach to each other. Start the project when they're fresh, either first thing on the agenda or just after a snack. Tempers are less likely to fly. Set up on a large table or floor with plenty of room between "artists." Roll out a large sheet of newsprint. You may choose to let the children create on their own or suggest some project from the outset (a fort, fire station, or airport). Guide and structure gently. After all, you're asking quite a lot of youngsters to collaborate. Finally, know when it's time to quit. Sometimes it's obvious—like the time Mitchell dumped the red paint on Naomi's head. But other times it's subtle. Any protests of termination will quickly fade as you hang the mural on the wall for glorious display!

Feather Painting

MATERIALS:

feathers/liquid tempera/muffin tins/large pieces of paper

Here's your chance to experiment with art and music. Turn on a classical record and allow the children to dip and paint with large sweeping motions on paper. You'll be amazed at the changes in style as the music rises and falls. Don't be afraid to discuss with the children how the music makes them feel. You might even suggest that they paint what they feel. Caution: Don't play the *William Tell* Overture or you may be surprised as Ann was when Jed galloped away with the dripping feather in hand.

Rock Painting

MATERIALS:

liquid tempera paint/assorted rocks/brushes/muffin tins

Once again, remember, painting is messy and, if possible, is best done outdoors. If not, pick an area where you will not be upset if paint is spilled. Kids sure do love to collect and paint rocks. For best results wash the rocks before painting. They make great paperweight gifts.

Straw Painting

MATERIALS:

straws/tempera paint/muffin tin/plastic spoons/paper

Pour a small amount of paint into the bottom of each muffin round. Three colors will create a beautiful variation in patterns. Have the children spoon a small amount of paint onto the paper. Now have the children blow through the straw spreading the paint in different directions.

Marble Painting

MATERIALS:

tempera paint/muffin tin/marbles/plastic spoons/colored construction paper/round tin container

The beautiful patterns formed by this art medium will surely awe both you and the children. Cut the construction paper to fit the bottom of the tin. Use a variety of colored construction paper to contrast with the color of the paints. Pour a small amount of paint into each muffin round, three different colors work best. Have the children place a marble in one of the paints. Remove the marble with a spoon, draining any excess paint. Place the marble in the tin and swirl the tin around and around in different directions. Repeat the procedure with other tempera colors.

Q-Tip Painting

MATERIALS:

Q-Tips/tempera paint/paper/muffin tin

Pour a small amount of paint into the bottom of each muffin round. Place a Q-Tip in each color. The children may proceed as if painting with a brush but make sure they understand they must replace the Q-Tip to the round in which they got it. The Q-Tips make bold, wide strokes that create an entirely different effect than brush strokes.

8

CLASSIFICATION AND DISCRIMINATION

THE MATCH GAME

Many matching and classification skills can be demonstrated through play. These tasks help children develop the ability to recognize likenesses and differences. This is the groundwork for later skills they need to distinguish between letters and eventually words. To learn to read and to do mathematics these visual discrimination skills must be well developed. Preschoolers naturally enjoy matching and sorting objects. Do as we did. Raid your local thrift shop and obtain a supply of buttons and hair curlers that the children can sort according to size, shape, and color; or set out items easily collected in the house. Card games and lotto games also improve discrimination skills. Here are some of the homemade games we developed.

Shape Match

MATERIALS:

5 of each of the following shapes—circle, square, rectangle, and triangle/large pieces of oak tag with a sample of each shape glued on them/shoe box

Put all the shapes into a shoe box. Have the children take turns picking a shape and matching it to the shape on the board. Have the children name the shape as they do the activity. Younger children do better if each shape is a different color. When they really start to master the task, try all the same color.

Button Sort

MATERIALS:

a collection of different size, shape buttons/small index cards with 3 or 4 button outlines of various sizes drawn on them

For this game, just place the buttons in a shoe box. Have each child select one card. Let fingers and brains rummage through the shoe box to find the button that is the same size and shape as the outline drawn on the card. When the card is complete, it's someone else's turn. Nothing says you can't help out a bit if help is needed.

Pattern Sort

MATERIALS:

colored building blocks/a large plastic bin

Let's go one step further: Match a color sequence. Just line up three blocks, each a different color. Place the remaining blocks in a bin. Ask the children to choose the same color blocks that you have picked. Once they have that, see if they can line up the blocks exactly like yours. If they master that, try increasing the number of blocks and the complexity of the pattern. Over a year's time, the line will get longer and longer.

Bottle Top Match

MATERIALS:

10 old plastic bottles of various sizes with screw-on tops/ large bin for storage/Magic Markers

What bottle is complete without a top? Take your ten plastic bottles and go to town with some Magic Markers creating clowns, policemen, firemen with matching caps before the children arrive. When they get there, take off the lids and explain how unhappy the people are since they lost their hats. With this little bit of drama, certainly your group will team up to find the appropriate caps for the bottles.

Card Sort

MATERIALS:

deck of playing cards minus the picture cards

Line up the number cards, two to ten, of one suit in a row. The remaining cards go face down. Have the children take turns choosing a card and placing it on the correct number. Simple and successful.

Wallpaper Match

MATERIALS:

pages of wallpaper from an old wallpaper book/shoe box

Choose five different patterns of wallpaper (stripes, checks, or other clear patterns). Cut five 4-inch squares from each pattern of wallpaper. Then place all the different squares in the shoe box. Now take turns picking a square and finding all the matches to that square. In this game you can discuss the texture, color, and line of each pattern. If the children say they want their rooms done in purple velveteen, don't get upset. Just move on to the next game.

Where Do They Live?

MATERIALS:

large picture of farm mounted on a piece of cardboard/ large picture of zoo mounted on a piece of cardboard/pictures of various farm animals and zoo animals

Have the kids get the animals back where they belong. Put the animal pictures in a shoe box. Let them take turns choosing an animal and placing it on the appropriate piece of cardboard. Discussions on zoos and farms are sure to follow.

Big and Little Game

MATERIALS:

3 shoe boxes/pictures of objects that are big and little/glue

Here's an easy one. Glue a picture of something big on one box and something little on another box. Place the rest of the big and little pictures in the third box. Have the children take turns choosing a picture and placing it in the correct box.

Size Game

MATERIALS:

crayons/large roll of paper/empty cans of different sizes

Roll out a large piece of paper. Trace each can bottom onto the paper. Next have the children color in each circle. Now line up the cans randomly in front of the paper and have the children place each can on the correct size circle.

Touch Game

MATERIALS:

square pieces of material 4 by 4 inches, 2 squares of each texture (for instance, velvet, fur, cotton)/a box/a scarf

Place all the sets of materials in a box. Cover the children's eyes with a scarf and let them explore the various textures with their hands. Now see if they can match the textured materials by using only their sense of touch.

What Belongs in the Room?

MATERIALS:

large pictures of individual rooms of a house/pictures of items that belong in each room/shoe boxes

If cleaning up the house were only this easy! Just mount a picture of each room on the front of a separate shoe box. Put all the individual pictures of items that belong in the rooms in a shoe box, for example, pictures of sinks, beds, ovens, toilets. Have the children take turns choosing a picture and then placing it in the appropriate box.

9

AUDITORY SKILLS

CAPTURING THEIR EYES AND EARS

Listening is a skill, and a particularly difficult one for a group of preschoolers to master. With our kids success was related to the quality and makeup of the material we presented. They had to be interesting and age appropriate in every way. We concentrated on finger plays, music, and stories. You'll probably find, as we did, that only experience will tell you when you've made a good selection, and there's a weeding-out process to developing your own repertoire. Here are the listening activities that most often captured our preschoolers' eyes and ears.

FINGER PLAYS

You probably know that a finger play is a short poem or song that is accompanied by descriptive finger movements. Children love to imitate the movements of an animal or object in a finger play. Marilyn was so good at these that our children just went

wild and insisted that they be repeated at home. So we met one afternoon specifically to learn them. And here's an extra. Many finger plays make a soothing bedtime activity as well as a great time filler for short trips in the car or long waits on the supermarket line. Two books we recommend are *The Little Puffin* by Elizabeth Matterson (Penguin Books, Puffin Books, 1969) and *My Big Book of Fingerplays* by Daphne Hogstrom (Golden Books, Western Publishers Company, 1974).

Here are some of our favorite simple finger plays.

Make a circle
Make a square

Now put your finger in the air
Make a rectangle
Make a triangle
Now let your fingers jingle jangle.

Open, shut them, Open, shut them.
Give them a little clap
Open, shut them, Open, shut them.
Put them on your lap.
Creep them, Creep them, Creep them
Right up to your chin
Open up your mouth
But don't let them in.

Five little monkeys jumping on the bed
one fell off and bumped his head
called the doctor and the doctor said
No more monkeys jumping on the bed!

So there were four little monkeys jumping on the bed
one fell off . . .

So there were three little monkeys jumping on the bed
one fell off . . .

So there were two little monkeys jumping on the bed
one fell off . . .

So there was one little monkey jumping on the bed
he fell off . . .

Where are the monkeys?
Here they are!

Itsy Bitsy Spider went up the water spout.
Down came the rain and washed the spider out.
Out came the sun and dried up all the rain.
And the Itsy Bitsy Spider went up the spout again.

I have two eyes one, two.
I can wink and so can you.

When my eyes are open I can see the light.
When my eyes are closed it's dark as night.

Fishes here, fishes there,
Fishes swimming everywhere.
Swimming up, swimming down,
Swimming, swimming all around.

MUSIC

Kids love music and it helps them interact as a group. Most children have an innate appreciation for song and learn basic rhythm quite naturally. Including movement with your music activity provides a good physical outlet for these energetic youngsters. During long winter playgroup sessions outdoor activities may be impossible. It sure helps to have a collection of records and musical activities on hand. When the group becomes restless, channel their energies into musical movement. Here are some easy-to-make instruments as well as a short listing of records, some musical games, and some of our basic musical moves.

INSTRUMENTS

Shakers

MATERIALS:

paper plates/Magic Markers/stapler/rice or beans for filling/funnel

First staple the paper plates together leaving a 2- to 3-inch opening. Have the children decorate the plates with Magic Markers.

Then help the children pour the filling through the funnel into the paper plates. Staple the shakers closed.

Variation. For similar instruments with different sounds and shapes, try these.

MATERIALS:

orange juice containers/oatmeal boxes/small film containers/rice or beans for filling/funnel/tape/glue

Using any type of bean or rice, fill the containers and tape or glue closed. The oatmeal or juice cans can be painted or covered with decorative colored paper.

Drums

MATERIALS:

unsharpened pencils/oatmeal boxes/long string/Magic Markers or paint/glue

Fasten a string through each oatmeal box so that the kids can wear them. Glue the top on the container and decorate with paint or Magic Markers. A miracle: A drum loud enough to satisfy them and quiet enough to preserve a parent's ears.

Rhythm Sticks

MATERIALS:

2 pieces of thin wood/tempera paint/sandpaper

Have the children sand the sticks as smooth as possible. Then have them paint the sticks with ordinary tempera paint. Be sure to sand down all the sharp points. And remind the kids that they each have a matching pair to tap together to avoid the temptation of dueling, stabbing, or spearing their compatriots.

Sandblocks

MATERIALS:

sandpaper/wooden blocks/glue

Wrap the sandpaper around the blocks and glue in place with white glue. Rubbing the blocks together produces a great sound. If the glue doesn't stick, try prefabbing a cover for your block by creating an appropriate cylinder of sandpaper with a stapler. Then just slip it on.

Cymbals

Have each child bang two pot lids together in time to the music.

RECORDS

There are many records available for young children. Here are the ones we especially liked for their simple songs and easy rhythm:

1. *"Burl Ives Sings Little White Duck and Other Songs." Columbia Records.*
2. *"Woody Guthrie's Children's Songs." Golden Records.*
3. *"Sesame Street." Children's Records of America.*
4. *"Mister Rogers Come On and Wake Up." Mr. Pickwick Records.*
5. *"Learning Basic Skills through Music, Volume 1"; "Homemade Band"; "Creative Movement and Rhythmic Exploration." Hap Palmer Records. Educational Activities. (Since these records are not usually found in any record store, here is the address from which they can be obtained: Freeport, New York, 11520.)*
6. *"And One and Two"; "You'll Sing a Song and I'll Sing a Song"; "Early Childhood Songs." Ella Jenkins Records. Educational Activities. (See address above.)*

MUSICAL MOVEMENT

Scarf and Streamer Dancing

Put on a lively record and encourage the kids to move their bodies freely to the music, raising and lowering their scarves and streamers as they dance. This little prop (2 feet long is a good size) really turned the kids on, and it's nearly impossible to hurt another youngster with one of these soft scarves or streamers.

Rhythm Clapping

Gather the children in a circle, put on a record with a definitive beat, and have the children keep time to the music by clapping. Some clap instruction may be needed at first. Although they've been doing it since age one, sometimes it's hard to make just the right noise.

Marching

Put on a lively marching record. Supply each child with a homemade instrument and let the parade begin. In the spring throw open the windows, turn up the music, and lead the children up the street. Marilyn tried this and the neighborhood joined in. A retired couple even invited the band in for refreshments.

Hobbyhorse Fun

MATERIALS:

3-foot, one-inch round dowel/heavy cardboard/stapler gun/ crayons or Magic Markers

Cut out two heavy pieces of cardboard in the shape of the

horse's head. Attach a head to each side of the dowel with a stapler gun in several locations. Then let the kids decorate the base with crayons or Magic Markers. Now all you need is galloping music and children's imagination and you have cowhands, circus riders, or horse racers. We hope you're enjoying this as much as we are.

MUSICAL CIRCLE GAMES

Everybody hold hands and here we go with a few of our favorite circle games.

"The Farmer in the Dell"

This is a game that is ideally suited for a large group of children. However, with some modification it can still be fun with four participants. Assemble the children in a circle on the floor and explain that this game is about living on a farm. After you decide which child will be what animal you are ready to begin. (For example, Joey is a farmer, Susie is a cat, Billy is a lamb, and Judy is a duck.) Now you are ready for the children to stand up and hold hands. Place the farmer in the middle of the circle and, moving in a counterclockwise direction, begin singing the song as follows:

The farmer in the dell
The farmer in the dell
Hi! ho! the derry oh,
The farmer in the dell.

After this verse have the children stop, drop hands, and clap while the following verse is said with the name of a different animal inserted each time. Thus,

The farmer takes the (cat, or the lamb, or the duck, etc.)
The farmer takes the (cat, etc.)
Hi! ho! the derry oh,
The farmer takes the (cat, etc.)

Continue in this way until all of the animals have been chosen by the farmer and are inside the circle. The game can then be repeated with different animals used each time. Not only is it fun, but it is a good memory task as well.

"Here We Go Looby Loo"

This old standby is even enjoyed by adults at square dances and local fairs. The game is a good way to introduce or explain various parts of the body. Have the children stand anywhere they wish and sing the verses below. You can mention any parts that you or the children wish, inserting them in the blanks. The rest of the words describe the actions that are necessary.

Here we go Looby Loo,
Here we go Looby Light
Here we go Looby Loo
All on a Saturday Night.

I put my (right hand, foot, left hand, foot, etc.) in
I put my (right hand, foot, left hand, foot, etc.) out;
I give my hand a shake, shake, shake,
And turn myself about.

Repeat Chorus.

Kids really love this circle game and really come up with interesting parts of the body to move. We had a good belly dancing lesson once trying to move only our stomachs!

"Ring around the Rosy"

This circle game can be played the usual way, or with a little imagination variations can be added. Here are two variations that we found were fun. The basic rhyme remains the same, as do the actions, but several activities can be added. Join hands with the children, and, moving in a counterclockwise direction, sing the song. Follow the actions that the words suggest.

Ring around the rosy,
A pocket full of poseys.
Hopscotch hopscotch
All fall down!

Variation 1. After the children have fallen down, have them try to get up with the aid of one hand. Then as they gain competence with this skill, try getting up without using their hands. This is admittedly very hard to do but the kids in our playgroup loved to keep trying!

Variation 2. Warn the children ahead of time that at the end of the rhyme you are going to give them an instruction. Play the game as usual, singing the last verse "All fall down," and then add an instruction such as "and touch your head," or "and put your finger on your nose," or "touch your knees," etc. This simple game then becomes a game to improve listening skills as well.

"The Mulberry Bush"

Most of us are probably familiar with this song and the actions that go along with it. For those of you who are rusty with the words, you will find them below. You can make up any action that you wish to accompany the words, or better yet, have the children make up actions with you. Join hands and, moving in a circle, sing the refrain.

Refrain:
Here we go round the mulberry bush, the mulberry bush, the mulberry bush.
Here we go round the mulberry bush, so early in the morning.

This is the way we wash our clothes, wash our clothes, wash our clothes.
This is the way we wash our clothes, so early Monday morning.

(Repeat Refrain)

This is the way we hang our clothes, hang our clothes, hang our clothes.
This is the way we hang our clothes, so early Tuesday morning.

(Repeat Refrain)

This is the way we mend our clothes . . . so early Wednesday morning.

This is the way we iron our clothes . . . so early Thursday morning.

This is the way we fold our clothes . . . so early Friday morning.

By the way, you can even make up your own words for the song to accompany any other activity you may be doing. For example, if you are planting a garden with the children you can work in words and motions that are used in gardening as follows: This is the way we dig the ground, water the plants, pull the weeds, and so on. If you have been talking about transportation you can include verses about driving a tractor, riding a bicycle, or flying a plane. This is a wonderful game for maximum motion, so you can use it when the kids are restless and need movement.

"If You're Wearing . . ."

Learning about colors can be enhanced by singing and playing this simple circle game with the children. Seat the children on the floor around you while you sing with them. The actions follow the words of the song. As you sing about each color, have the child or children wearing that color do the action you have sung.

If you're wearing red, if you're wearing red
put your finger (or hand, thumb, pinkie) on your head.

If you're wearing blue, if you're wearing blue
put your finger on your shoe.

If you're wearing green, if you're wearing green
Wave your hand so you can be seen.

If you're wearing brown, if you're wearing brown
Show us a very very very mean frown.

If you're wearing yellow, if you're wearing yellow
Make yourself into a very funny fellow.

You can make up any other verses you can think of with various other colors.

"I'm Selling Lollipops"

This is another color recognition game. To play this game you need to make "lollipops" from cardboard, or you can use tongue depressors that you color at one end. Have the children seated in a circle on the floor and walk in between them singing the following song.

I'm selling lollipops
Sugar coated lollipops

I'm selling lollipops
Nobody knows where I will stop.

At the word "stop" have the child nearest you choose a lollipop. Ask the child to tell you the color. See if the child can find something else in the room that is the same color. Let the child keep the "lollipop" and begin the game again. When the children have become familiar with the game allow them to take turns being the lollipop man or woman. For a special treat, this game can be played with real lollipops.

Variation. This variation of the game can be played with the children as they are gaining competency in number and letter recognition. In addition to the color on the "lollipop" that you make, add either a number or a letter. Then when you sing your song and stop at a child, have the child tell you the color of the "lollipop" as well as the number or letter that appears on it.

"I'm a Little Teapot"

This old English folk song is a great one to do outside on a cold winter day. By blowing steam from their mouths the children can pretend they are teapots "hot and ready."

I'm a little teapot short and stout.
Here is my handle, here is my spout.
When I'm full and ready, here me shout.
Tip me over and pour me out.

"Muffin Man"

This is another old English folk song with very simple lyrics. Have the children face each other, the first group singing the first verse and the second group responding with the second verse.

Oh! Do you know the muffin man, the muffin man, the muffin man.
Do you know the muffin man who lives on Cherry Lane.
Oh, Yes we know the muffin man, the muffin man, the muffin man.
Yes we know the muffin man who lives on Cherry Lane.

Now that you have read through some of our most popular musical games, you might wish to enlarge your repertoire. Remember that singing, moving, and clapping your hands to the music with young children is enough to constitute a game or dance. Below is a listing of recommended music books with a description of their content.

Tom Glazer's Treasury of Folk Songs. Compiled by Tom Glazer. Grosset & Dunlap, 1964. (This anthology of folk songs contains the well-known classics including "The Farmer in the Dell" and "The Mulberry Bush.")

Heritage Songster. Lion and Lynn Dallin. Brown, 1972. (This is another folk song anthology that also contains the old favorites including "The Farmer in the Dell" and "The Mulberry Bush.")

Eve Winker, Tom Tinker, Chin Chopper. Tom Glazer. Doubleday, 1973. (This is a very good small collection of fingerplays including Itsy Bitsy Spider [Tom Glazer's version uses Eensy Weensy Spider] set to music with chords for piano and guitar.)

Wake Up and Sing. Elizabeth Crook and Beatrice Landeck. Edward B. Marks Music Corp., Morrow, 1969. (A collection of not-so-well-known children's songs with easy piano arrangements that is organized according to various themes. These include awareness of self, awareness of environment, awareness of rhythm, etc.)

This Little Puffin. Compiled by Elizabeth Matterson. Penguin Books Ltd., 1971. (An excellent collection of fingerplays and short, easy songs arranged for piano and organized into categories such as in the house, in the zoo, birds and animals, etc.)

Favorite Nursery Rhymes. Compiled by Phyllis Brown Ohanian. Random House, 1956. (A collection of favorite nursery rhymes that are set to music with easy piano and guitar arrangements, including "The Farmer in the Dell," "Ring Around the Rosy," "Here We Go Looby Loo," and "The Mulberry Bush.")

More Songs to Grow On. Beatrice Landeck. Edward B. Marks Music Co., William Sloane Associates, Inc., 1954. (Another collection of simple but not well-known children's songs organized into various categories such as the animal kingdom, singing games and rounds, dramatic play songs, festive and carol songs, etc.)

The Fireside Book of Children's Songs. Collected and Edited by Marie Winn. Simon & Schuster, 1966. (A collection of folk songs primarily for children, this too is divided into categories including silly songs, nursery songs, birds and beasts, good morning and good night, and singing games and rounds. This collection contains many songs that are not found in the above-mentioned folk song collections. The music is simply arranged for piano or guitar.)

STORIES

One of the most relaxing and enjoyable activities for preschoolers is story time. A good time for a story is after snack. Just gather everyone in front of you on the floor. Not everyone will come. Some may wish to sit apart and do a quiet activity on their own, and that's all right. Sit facing the children, holding the book so that they can see the pictures as you read the text. Always familiarize yourself with the book before reading it out loud. Choose stories that are age appropriate or you'll quickly have a bored and inattentive audience.

When choosing books for young children, one needs to consider many items: Length of story, words per page, type of illustrations, and topic. Choose a story containing fifteen to twenty pages depending upon the text. Young children will lose interest if the wording is too complex or the text is too long. Use your judgment. If you notice that the children are drifting, paraphrase the material as you read. Young children delight in bold, simple, and defined illustrations. Stay away from abstract, whimsical drawings that might appeal to you as an adult, but are not clearly defined for your child.

What topics are best? We found that the categories of animals, transportation, people, and seasons appeal most to the

preschooler. In addition, certain stories lend themselves better to reading for a group than others. We have included a list of preschool stories that were some of the kids' favorites. But don't stop here. Go to your own neighborhood library and see what their preschool section has to offer.

Alexander, Martha. *Sabrina.* Dial Press, 1971. (A little girl, Sabrina, thinks everyone is making fun of her name and then realizes how pretty and desirable it really is.)

——. *The Story Grandmother Told.* Dial Press, 1969. (Lisa tells her grandmother her favorite story and then wants her to retell it.)

Banner, Angela. *The Ant and the Bee and the Rainbow.* Kaye and Ward, 1972. (A super book on colors.)

Barrett, Judi. *Peter's Pocket.* Atheneum, 1974. (Peter's mom cleverly solves the problem of Peter's love for pockets.)

Brown, Margaret Wise. *Color Kitten.* Golden, 1958. (This is a standard book for introducing colors.)

——. *Goodnight Moon.* Harper & Row, 1947. (A bedtime story about a little rabbit saying good night to everything in his bedroom.)

——. *The Little Fireman.* William. R. Scott Inc., 1938. (The story of a big fireman and a little fireman.)

——. *The Noisy Book.* Harper & Row, 1939. (A little dog named Muffin hears noises all around him.)

——. *The Runaway Bunny.* Harper & Row, 1972. (This is a good parental reassurance book.)

Bruna, Dick. *The Egg.* Follett, 1975. (This is a story about the hatching of a duckling.)

——. *Miffy in the Snow.* Follett, 1975. (Miffy helps save a bird during a snowstorm.)

——. *Miffy's Birthday.* Follett, 1976. (A little rabbit named Miffy celebrates her birthday.)

——. *The Sailor.* Follett, 1979. (A sailor goes to sea and has many adventures.)

Note: All of the books in this Bruna series are excellent for two-year-olds. They are short, with simple, bold illustrations.

Buckley, Helen. *Josie and the Snow.* Lothrop, 1966. (A little girl and her family have fun in the snow.)

——. *Josie's Buttercup.* Lothrup, 1967. (A rhyming story about Josie and her dog Buttercup.)

Carle, Eric. *The Hungry Caterpillar.* World, 1970. (A well-illustrated and easy first science book about the life of a caterpillar.)

Carlson, Dale and Al Carlson. *Good Morning Danny.* Atheneum, 1972. (The daily adventures of a little boy who is almost three.)

——. *Good Morning Hannah.* Atheneum, 1972. (The daily adventures of a little girl who is almost three.)

Ets, Marie Hal. *In the Forest.* Viking, 1944. (A little boy takes a walk in the forest and lets his imagination wander.)

——. *Just Me.* Viking, 1965. (A little boy pretends to be like his animal friends.)

——. *Play with Me.* Viking, 1955. (A little girl goes to the meadow to play with the animals.)

Flack, Marjorie. *Angus and the Cat.* Doubleday, 1932. (Angus, a Scottish terrier, learns to get along with the family cat.)

——. *Angus and the Ducks.* Doubleday, 1930. (Angus's curiosity about the neighboring ducks gets him into trouble.)

——. *Angus Lost.* Doubleday, 1932. (One cold morning Angus follows a milk truck and gets lost.)

——. *Ask Mr. Bear.* Macmillan, 1932. (A little boy tries to find a gift for his mother's birthday and is helped by a bear.)

Fleuridas, Ellie. *I Learn to Swim.* Macmillan, 1962. (A simple, reassuring story about children becoming comfortable in the water and gradually learning to swim.)

Foster, Joanna. *Pete's Puddle.* Harcourt Brace Jovanovich, 1969. (A little boy dressed for rain has fun playing in mud puddles.)

Freeman, Don. *Beady Bear.* Viking, 1954. (A wind-up bear discovers there is no place like home.)

——. *Corduroy.* Viking, 1968. (A tender story of a little girl and a toy bear who find each other in a department store.)

——. *Dandelion.* Viking, 1964. (A lion dresses up for party only to discover that no one recognizes him.)

Hoban, Tana. *Circles, Triangles, and Squares.* Macmillan, 1974.

——. *Is It Red? Is It Yellow? Is It Blue? An adventure in color.* Greenwillow, 1978.

——. *Push-Pull Empty-Full. A Book of Opposites.* Macmillan, 1972.

This series of books concerns itself with early concept learning. All the books are illustrated with photographs taken from everyday life scenes.

Hutchins, Pat. *Goodnight Owl.* Macmillan, 1972. (After all the animals keep Mr. Owl up during the day, he takes his revenge at nightfall.)

——. *Titch.* Macmillan, 1971. (A little girl discovers that having something small sometimes can be rewarding.)

——. *Rosie's Walk.* Macmillan, 1968. (A boldly illustrated, humorous, but simple story of a hen out for walk, eagerly pursued by a fox.)

Keats, Ezra Jack. *Over in the Meadow.* Four Winds Press, 1971. (A lovely rendition of the old song/poem.)

——. *Peter's Chair.* Harper & Row, 1967. (Peter learns in the end how to part with his baby things and then helps to ready them for his baby sister.)

——. *Snowy Day.* Viking, 1962. (A good story for a first day of snow about the fun it can bring.)

——. *Whistle for Willie.* Viking, 1964. (A little boy, Pete, triumphantly learns how to whistle.)

Kessler, Ethel and Leonard Kessler. *All Aboard the Train.* Doubleday, 1964. (This is a rhythmic story of a train ride.)

Krauss, Ruth. *Carrot Seed.* Harper & Row, 1945. (With caring and perseverance a little boy manages to grow his carrot against all the admonitions of his family.)

Dr. Seuss. *ABC Book.* Random House, 1963. (Dr. Seuss introduces the alphabet using rhyming words.)

Rockwell, Anne. *I Like the Library.* Dutton, 1977.

——. *Toolbox.* Macmillan, 1971.

Rockwell, Harlow. *My Dentist.* Greenwillow, 1975.

——. *My Doctor.* Macmillan, 1973.

——. *My Kitchen.* Greenwillow, 1980.

——. *My Nursery School.* Greenwillow, 1976.

Rockwell, Anne and Harlow Rockwell. *The Supermarket.* Macmillan, 1979.

All of the Rockwell books that are listed above are written in a similar style. They are designed to impart information about everyday items in the young child's environment in an easy-to-understand way and are illustrated with simple and accurate drawings of the subject matter.

Steiner, Charlotte. *My Slippers Are Red.* Knopf, 1957. (The children fill in the missing color as you read the rhyming verses.)

Tison, Annette and Talus Taylor. *Barbapapa's Ark.* Scholastic Book Services, 1974. (A fanciful and colorful story about respecting the plants and creatures of our environment.)

Welber, Robert. *A Winter Picnic.* Pantheon, 1970. (A little boy convinces his busy mother to take time out for a picnic in the snow.)

Wolde, Gunilla. *Betsy and Peter Are Different.* Random House, 1979. (The book discusses how Betsy and Peter are different in many ways but how much fun the differences provide.)

——. *This Is Betsy.* Random House, 1975. (A delightful story that depicts the two ways Betsy does routine things, correctly and humorously.)

——. *Tommy and Sarah Dress Up.* Mifflin Press, 1972. (The adventures of two children and a trunk of old clothes.)

——. *Tommy Builds a House.* Mifflin Press, 1971. (Tommy builds a house and invites his mommy and daddy in for a party.)

——. *Tommy Cleans His Room.* Houghton Mifflin, 1971. (While Tommy searches for his brown bear he also manages to clean his room.)

10

OBSERVATION AND PARTICIPATION

EDIBLE DELIGHTS

Cooking provides a multitude of experiences for youngsters. It combines observation with participation. Allow the children to pour, mix, and fill according to the specific requirements of the recipe. Anything they are not capable of doing should be done beforehand. It's best to premeasure the ingredients. You can point out the unit of measure as they pour and mix it. Even with these preparations expect a big mess!

When you cook with children you involve many of their senses. Feeling the texture of cookie dough, smelling the ingredients of applesauce, listening to the sounds of popcorn pop, watching the egg whites form stiff peaks, all make your children's senses stand up and say "wow." Look at their eyes. You know that they are having fun. Possibly the most important aspect of cooking with young children is their sense of accomplishment from making and sharing what they've prepared. Here are some edible delights for young preschoolers. Be sure to leave enough batter in the bowl for a taste. It's the best part.

Banana-on-a-Stick

INGREDIENTS:

bananas/vanilla wafers or graham crackers/peanut butter/ raw sunflower seeds/popsicle sticks/wax paper

Begin by having the children fill small paper sacks with four or five cookies. Secure the tops of the bags by folding them down several times and stapling. Allow the children to crush the cookies with their hands or feet or with rolling pins, hammers, or other suitable objects. Then add the raw sunflower seeds to the cookie crumbs and pour the mixture onto wax paper. Peel the bananas, have the children cut them in half, and spread peanut butter on all sides. Roll each banana half into the nut and crumb mixture until it is coated. Insert a popsicle stick into the center of the banana piece and refrigerate until snack time. Munch your bananas-on-a-stick while reading a good story about monkeys!

Roll-Pat Cookies

INGREDIENTS:

1 C Bisquick/1 small box of chocolate pudding/¼ C oil/ 1 egg

Mix all the ingredients together in a bowl. Shape the dough into balls. Bake at 375° for eight to ten minutes.

No-Bake Cookies—Variation 1

INGREDIENTS:

12 oz. butterscotch pieces/30 oz. can chow mein noodles/ 1 C salted peanuts

Melt the butterscotch pieces over hot water. Remove the pot and stir in noodles and peanuts. Drop by the spoonfuls and cool on wax paper. The chances of any arriving home are slim.

No-Bake Cookies—Variation 2

INGREDIENTS:

2 C sugar/½ C milk/¼ lb. butter/5 T cocoa/2½ C Quick Oats/1 t vanilla

Mix the sugar, milk, butter, and cocoa. Bring to a boil and cook for 1½ minutes. Remove and add vanilla and oatmeal. Beat till stiff and drop on waxed paper by the spoonful. Cool. Cookies for the child with a sweet tooth!

Graham Cracker No-Bake Cookies

INGREDIENTS:

½ C raisins/½ C chopped dates/2 T honey/graham crackers

Pour the raisins, dates, and honey into a mixing bowl. Place several graham crackers in a plastic bag and crush them with a rolling pin. Add this to the honey-fruit mixture until it's dry enough to roll into balls. Delicious and healthy too.

Easy Roll-Out Cookie Dough

INGREDIENTS:

½ C shortening/1 C granulated sugar/1 t vanilla/1 egg/2 C sifted all-purpose flour/½ t baking powder/¼ t salt

Thoroughly mix shortening, sugar, and vanilla. Add egg and beat till light and fluffy. Sift together the dry ingredients and blend into creamed mixture. Divide dough in half. Chill one hour. On lightly floured surface, roll to 1/8-inch thickness. Cut into desired shapes with cutter. Bake on greased cookie sheet at 375° for about six to eight minutes. Cool slightly, remove from pan. Makes two dozen. For fun have a variety of cookie cutters available and let the children pick their own shapes.

Cookie Paint—Variation 1

INGREDIENTS:

evaporated milk/food coloring/several small paper cups/ pastry brushes

Place small amount of evaporated milk into separate small cups. Tint with different colors using food coloring. With a small brush paint the cookies. It hardly seems right to eat a green cookie, but kids'll do it every time.

Cookie Paint—Variation 2

INGREDIENTS:

egg yolks/food coloring/small dishes/pastry brush

Beat egg yolks with food coloring. Pour into little dishes and, using small brushes, paint the tops of the cookies. This is for your cookie painter who desires a lighter stroke from the pleasantly palatable paint than can be achieved with Cookie Paint 1.

Peanut Butter Cookies

INGREDIENTS:

1 C smooth peanut butter/½ C honey/½ C dry milk

Mix all ingredients together. Have the children mold the dough into balls. Refrigerate for an hour. Now there's an easy one and good too.

Jell-O Shapes

INGREDIENTS:

4 envelopes of Knox unflavored gelatin/3 packages (3 oz. each) flavored gelatin/4 C boiling water

In a large bowl combine unflavored and flavored gelatin. Add boiling water and stir till dissolved. Pour into shallow pan and chill until firm. Using cookie cutters cut into shapes. Decorate if desired. Our kids had the greatest fun with this recipe on Valentine's Day. We made cherry-flavored gelatin, got out the heart-shaped cookie cutters, and created a holiday snack. A little spurt of whipped cream adds the special touch. (This recipe is used courtesy of Knox Gelatine, Inc.)

Cinnamon Toast

INGREDIENTS:

any bread toasted/butter or margarine/1 t cinnamon/½ C sugar

Mix the cinnamon and sugar together. Have the bread already toasted. Let the children spread margarine on the bread. Using shakers (any small containers with holes on the top) have the children shake a mixture of sugar and cinnamon on the toast. Note: Parents are allowed to indulge too.

Popcorn

INGREDIENTS:

popcorn/oil/salt

Follow the directions on popcorn maker or package. It's best on a cold, windy, damp day. For especially festive moods try colored popcorn.

Peanut Butter

INGREDIENTS:

2 C peanuts/2 T oil/salt

Crack the peanut shells slightly so that the children can remove them more easily. Put the peanuts in a blender, add 2 tablespoons of oil and salt to taste. Blend till smooth. Here's a good chance for you to discuss how other foods we buy in the supermarket are made.

Stuffed Celery

INGREDIENTS:

several stalks of celery/peanut butter/cream cheese/any other spread

Have the children cut the celery into pieces and fill it with cream cheese, peanut butter, or any other spread. Mitchell's favorite was celery lined with peanut butter and topped with raisins. He called it "Ants on the Log."

Banana Dunk Dip

INGREDIENTS:

bananas/½ C jelly/½ C chocolate syrup/½ C whipped cream

Have the children cut the bananas into one-inch sections. Arrange jelly, chocolate syrup, whipped cream in small bowls. Dip the bananas into the different bowls. And voilà! Banana fondue à la playgroup!

One-Rise Buttermilk Bread

INGREDIENTS:

2 packages yeast/¾ C warm milk/1½ C buttermilk (or one cup of sweet milk + one T lemon juice)/4½ C to 5 C flour/

½ C shortening/2 T sugar/2 t salt/2 t baking powder/disposable aluminum potato shells

Dissolve yeast in warm water. Add the buttermilk, 2½ C flour, shortening, sugar, salt, and baking powder. Beat for one-half minute at low speed and two minutes at high speed. Add the rest of the flour and knead for five minutes. Divide the dough into small loaf shapes. We baked the dough in disposable aluminum potato shells purchased at the local supermarket. The dough should be about the size of a small potato. Let the dough rise for one hour in a warm place. Preheat oven at 425°. Bake at 425° for twenty-five to thirty minutes. We can't tell you how thrilled the children were to bring home loaves of bread to share with their families. And when they made their lunch—peanut butter and jelly sandwiches on homemade bread—their chests heaved with pride!

Applesauce

INGREDIENTS:

6 apples/½ C water/1 t cinnamon/2 T sugar

Peel the apples. Remove the cores. Cut the apples into quarters. Cook apples in water. Drain the apples. Then add the sugar and cinnamon. Cook till soft and tender. It's yummy warm!

Cheese Sandwiches

INGREDIENTS:

American cheese slices/bread slices/cookie cutter/raisins/nuts

Here's one we loved. Have the children cut the cheese and the bread with their favorite cookie cutter. Place the cheese shape on the bread shape. Decorate with nuts or raisins for appropriate eyes, buttons, or whatever. Now you've got to admit that's a great idea, and so simple. Good for a birthday lunch!

Orange Delight

INGREDIENTS:

6 oz. can frozen orange juice/1¾ C water/½ C dry milk/¼ C sugar/12 ice cubes/1 t vanilla

Pour all the ingredients into a blender and blend at high speed until frothy. The kids can take turns pushing the buttons on your blender. They can't hurt the blender, and all the blades are well hidden.

Berry Delicious

INGREDIENTS:

1 quart milk/1½ C strawberries or any other fruit/2 T sugar

Pour all the ingredients into a blender. Blend until well mixed. Drink and say "moo."

Note: Both these drinks are nutritious, refreshing pick-me-ups on a warm playgroup day.

11

APPRECIATION OF THE ENVIRONMENT

OUTDOOR ACTIVITIES AND EXCURSIONS

Whenever possible, spend a portion of your activity time outside. It usually works well to schedule the outdoor play toward the end of the playgroup period when the children are apt to be feeling a little frisky. Freedom of space helps them settle down. In very nice weather, indoor activities may be moved outdoors as well. For example, finger painting, snack time, or story time, under a big tree. This provides a pleasant change of pace. These outdoor activities and play equipment have worked best for us.

THE GREAT OUTDOORS

Sand Play

MATERIALS:

sandbox (store-bought or homemade; 5 by 5 feet seems to be a good size)/sand (this can be purchased inexpensively at a construction company if you are willing to shovel it into your car yourself)/sand toys (shovels, pails, strainers, trucks, old spoons, cups, funnels, rakes, and hoes)

Sand play is a very soothing and relaxing activity for young children. It lends itself to group play as well as individual play. With the appropriate equipment the children can practice the skills of pouring, sifting, measuring, stirring to their hearts' content and there's no need to worry about spills. It's also great for the imagination. On the other hand, a little surveillance from a distance is always useful. Somehow our kids always felt it was a great idea to play shower in the sandbox.

Water Play

MATERIALS:

large pool/water toys (pans, ladles, cups, squeeze bottles, sponges)

Give the kids objects that float and toys for spilling and filling such as pots and pans. Then let them enjoy this refreshing activity. And pouring is so great for eye-hand coordination!

Ball Toss

MATERIALS:

large ball/orange crate

Give each child a few turns tossing the ball and trying to get it in the crate. Large arm muscles as well as eye-hand coordination benefit. Large balls are best. If someone's upset at missing, let them kick the ball. It's the ball's fault, anyway!

Rope Jump

Place a jump rope or a large thick cord on the ground. Have the children take turns trying to jump over the rope without landing on it. This game helps the children use and strengthen leg muscles and also improves coordination and balance. Actual conventional jump roping is probably hard for preschoolers. But if you have that special talent in your group, give it a try.

Hula Hoop Jump

Here's a good jumping game for tots. Have the kids jump in and out of the hula hoop one at a time, trying not to land on the rim. This is a variation of rope jumping that strengthens muscles and improves coordination and balance.

Bean Bag Toss

MATERIALS:
hula hoop/bean bags

Have the children stand around the rim of the hula hoop and toss the bean bags into the hoop. As their coordination improves, increase the distance between them and the hoop. Some will do better than others, and attention span varies here. Make it easy enough for everyone to succeed initially.

Gardening

Children love all aspects of nature. A wonderful spring activity is to set aside a small plot for the children to plant a garden. The initial preparation such as plowing, fertilizing, and hoeing can be done without the children. Choosing and planting the seeds would be a full morning experience for the group. You might want to buy some starter plants so the children can see their efforts blossom sooner. In the weeks and months to come the children can share the experience of weeding, watering, and watching their plants grow and then delight in preparing nutritional snacks from the garden.

Water Painting

MATERIALS:

a bucket of water/paintbrushes—2-3 inches wide

Using just water and paintbrushes the children can make designs on the sidewalk or pretend they're painting the house, car, or any other outdoor surface. The great part about this activity is that there is positively no mess!

OUTDOOR PLAY EQUIPMENT

As young parents we admired the variety of creative playgrounds that were being constructed at area schools. There has been a trend away from standard metal playgrounds toward constructions that not only complement the environment but also encourage creative play by the children and make use of their large motor muscles (i.e., crawling, climbing, stretching, jumping).

Standard metal equipment available at many large stores provides for standard types of exercise. The less expensive models tend to be lightweight, to be less durable, and to weather poorly. Well-designed, weatherproof, creative wooden swing sets are available that combine swings, ladder climbs, jungle gym,

slide, and climbing ropes. The Childlife Company in Holliston, Massachusetts provides a brochure and price list on request. For young families such as ours, however, cost became a prominent factor.

After some searching we found that the raw materials for a playground could be obtained for little or no cost. Intermittent trips to the local telephone company surplus yard provided an ample supply of used electrical spools in a variety of sizes, 3-foot, 1-by-4 planks from old broken spools, old 4-by-4 wooden studs (approximately 12 feet long), and all types of nuts and bolts. A second stop at the local junkyard or auto body shop supplied us with old car and truck tires. At small expense, other necessary objects such as supplemental hardware, chains, or sheet metal were purchased. With these basic and mostly free supplies we were able to build our playground.

If you wish to take the responsibility of creating a playground you must keep in mind safety and the need for supervision. The surface area should be well covered with sand. This may be inexpensively purchased in bulk from a construction company that delivers by the truckload. It is even less expensive to pick up the sand yourself. We covered the trunk of one car with an old blanket and shoveled the sand into it for practically nothing. The sand provides a soft place for the children to land if they fall and seconds as a giant sandbox. When determining the height of different equipment, keep in mind the ages of the children and their capabilities. Any raised platforms, bridges, or slides must have railings to prevent tumbles. All bolts used in construction must be flush with the surfaces, to avoid tripping and scrapes. You may have to use a hacksaw to cut surplus bolts down to size or you may wish simply to purchase the correct size.

A word about supervision. A free and imaginative playground that encourages creativity requires a watchful adult eye, but if it is constructed properly, young children ought to be able to move about in it freely and safely with only minimal intervention. Here are some of our creative constructions:

Balance Beam

MATERIALS:

one 4-by-4 plank (8 to 12 feet long)/2 2-foot, 4-by-4 pieces/ 20 pennyweight galvanized nails or 6-inch-long, 3/8-inch lag bolt/hammer, wrench, drill/

One foot from either end of the 4-by-4 plank, attach a 2-foot piece horizontally with either twenty pennyweight nails or a 6-inch, 3/8-lag bolt (prior drill hole required). The small pieces lay on the ground and provide both some height and stability for the beam. Once the beam is constructed, the children take turns trying to cross without falling. They often mimic tightrope walkers, stepping in short, careful motions forward and backward. The activity is fun and is useful for balance and coordination.

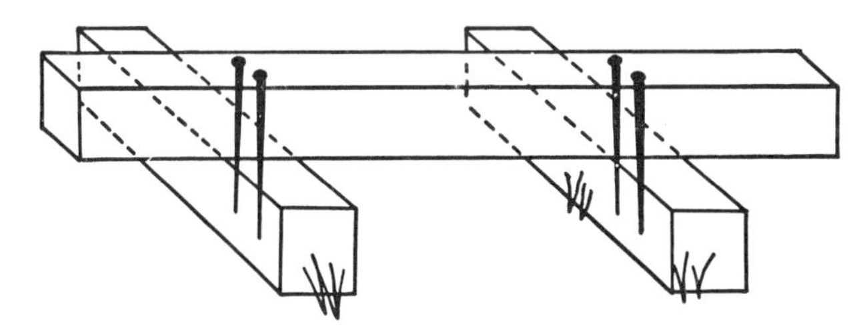

Tire Swing

MATERIALS:

heavy swing rope/large tire, preferably non-steel belted, non-snow tire, bald/circular saw, jigsaw, or hacksaw

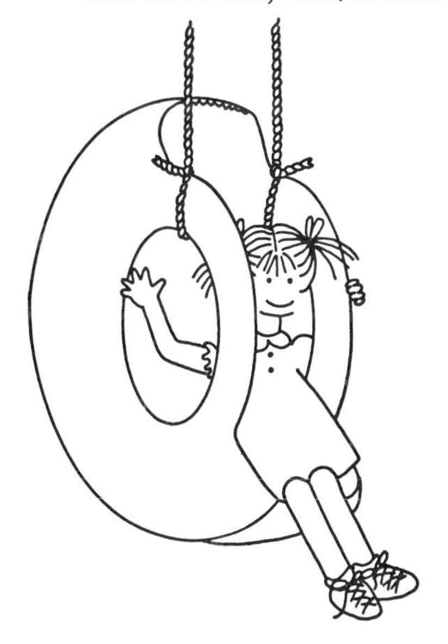

With a circular saw, jigsaw, or hacksaw cut out tire according to illustration. Then turn tire inside out. This provides extra interior space. Attach to swing rope as shown.

Tire Tunnel

MATERIALS:

6 large tires of roughly the same size/shovel

Dig a ditch deep enough to allow a tire standing up on end to be one-third below ground surface. The ditch should be wide enough to allow the tire to fit in crossways. Arrange tires 6 inches apart from each other and then cover lower portions with dirt so that the lower inner rim is just buried. Pack in dirt tightly with shovel or foot so that tires are immovable.

Tire Sandbox

Lay a large truck tire flat on the ground and fill it with sand.

Spool Table and Chairs

MATERIALS:

1 medium-size spool/4 small spools/wood preservative

Paint all exposed wood with wood preservative. Lay spools with flat surface down, arranging small spools around the large spool. The surfaces of the table and chairs may be covered with removable weatherproof tablecloth and cushions.

Spool Bridge

MATERIALS:

10 8-foot 2-by-4s/2 large spools of same size/wood preservative/approximately 30 feet of heavy-duty chain/35 3-foot pieces of 1-by-4s/surplus nuts and bolts/heavy-duty rope (about 30 feet)

Weatherize all exposed wooden surfaces. Set the spools, flat side down, 12 feet apart from each other. Drill two holes in each spool 30 inches apart as illustrated. Attach chains beneath lip of spools by bolts as shown. Drill holes in 1-by-4 planks 3 inches from either end. Attach planks to chain by inserting bolts through wood and chain hole and then tightening nuts from below. Use bolt cutter or hacksaw to remove any excess bolt exposed below. Attach 2-by-4 planks with nails to spool as illustrated in drawing, drilling a hole through the 2-by-4 at a point approximately 2 feet above the top surface of the spool. String rope through holes as illustrated to form protective rope railing. Always have the children hold the railing when crossing the bridge. A railing plank or ladder provides entrance to the spool as illustrated.

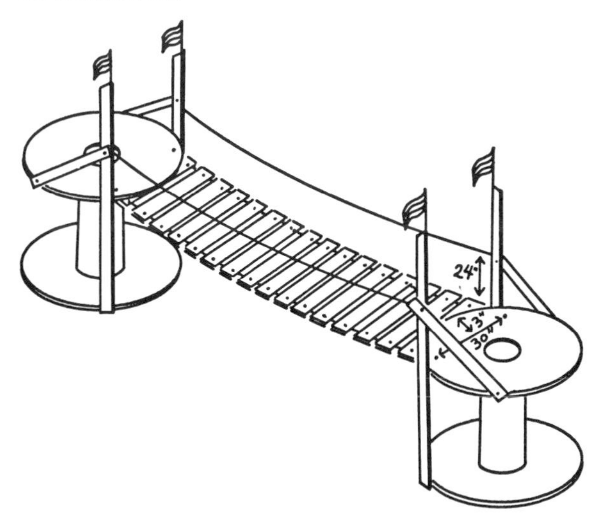

Spool Fort

MATERIALS:

giant spool/approximately 30 3-foot 1-by-4s/nails/wood preservative

Paint all exposed wood with wood preservative. Lie spool with flat surface down. Attach 1-by-4s to upper and lower lips as shown leaving a 2-foot exposed entryway. Using a jigsaw you may wish to cut out 6-inch-by-6-inch view ports or 12-inch-by-12-inch windows as illustrated. These will require framing in by a cross board as illustrated.

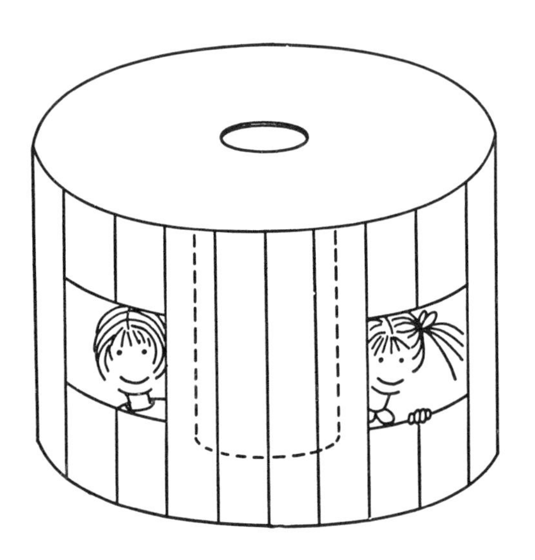

Elevated Walkway

MATERIALS:

2 large spools/2 12-foot 4-by-4s/surplus nuts and bolts/10 2-by-4s/25 feet of rope or 35 1-by-4s for railing/35 1-by-4s for bridge planks/wood preservative

Weatherize all wood surfaces. Place spools 10 feet apart. Drill two holes 30 inches apart on each spool as illustrated. Drill hole 6 inches from either end of 2 12-foot 4-by-4s. Attach 4-by-4s to undersurface of upper lip of spool with 8-inch bolts. Nail 1-by-4s flush with each other to 4-by-4 bridge as shown. Attach 2-by-4s to spools and bridge as illustrated. Use rope or 1-by-4s for a railing. A plank or ladder provides access to the bridge.

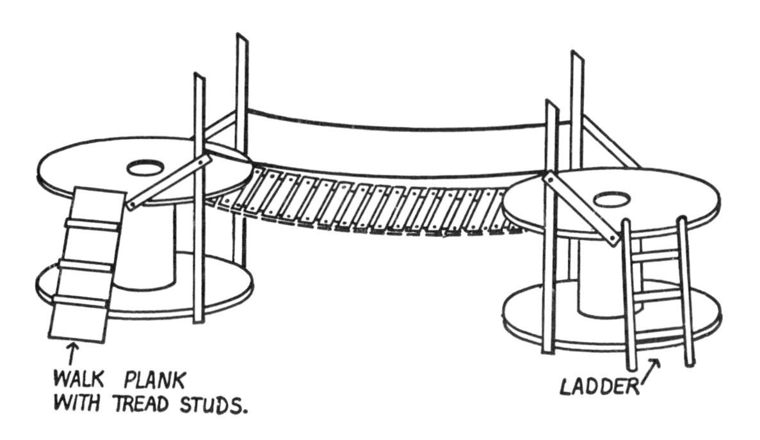

Spool Slide

MATERIALS:

large spool/2 4-by-4s/8-by-6 foot sheet of heavy-gauge sheet metal/32 feet of 1-by-3 fir stripping/3 2-by-4s/wood preservative/surplus bolts

Weatherize all wood with wood preservative. Place the spool on its flat surface. One of the existing spools from the chain bridge or elevated walkway may be used for slide platform. Drill two holes 4 feet apart as illustrated. Cut 2 4-by-4s to be approximately 18 inches longer than the sheet metal. Bend the sheet metal around three edges of the 4-by-4s with the 4-by-4s being 4 feet apart; nail in place over 1-by-3 fir stripping, flush with the end of the 4-by-4s at one end. Reinforce back of slide with 3 4-foot pieces of 2-by-4s. Drill a hole 6 inches from the exposed end of each 4-by-4. Connect slide to spool with bolts. Extra-long bolts may be required because of the angle connection.

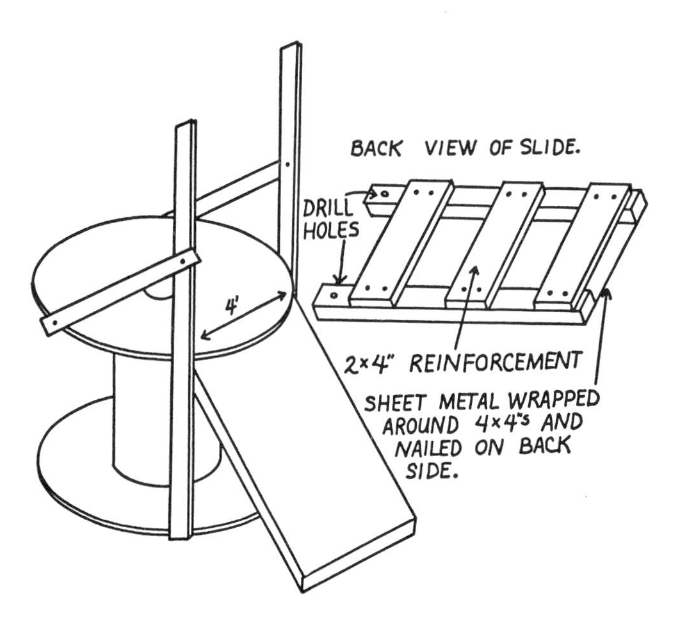

Buried Logs

MATERIALS:

6 large (1- to 2-foot diameter) logs of varying lengths/shovel

Dig a large hole deep enough to bury your largest log halfway. Arrange logs, standing, side by side so that they provide an uneven steplike platform. Adjust each log, filling in dirt underneath where necessary, so that it is half buried. Pound dirt in place around and between logs so that the entire structure is sturdy. Children of all ages enjoy climbing and jumping up and down on this log platform.

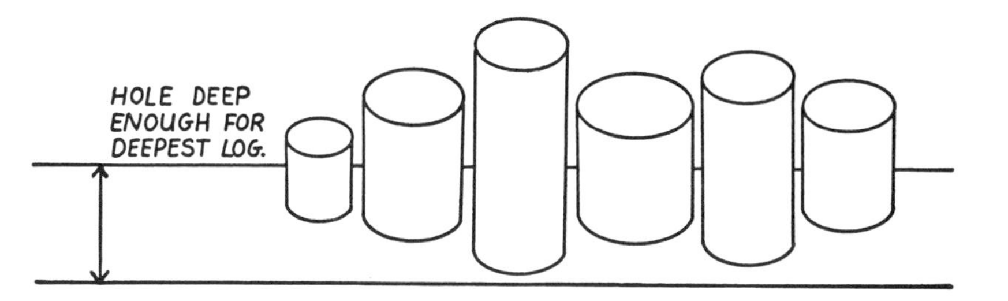

Fishnet or Rope-mesh Climbers

MATERIALS:

fishnet or old rope hammock/4 wooden or metal stakes/3-foot pieces of 2-by-4s/drill/bolts

Secure climber to ground and platform above. A spool may serve as the platform. Fold one end of the fishnet or rope-mesh over a 3-foot piece of 2-by-4. Temporarily nail the 2-by-4 to the platform. Then make three drill holes through the 2-by-4 and underlying platform and permanently join the two with bolts. Then stretch the climber tight and secure it to the ground with long metal or wooden stakes.

Monkey Seat or Rope Seat

MATERIALS:

thick rope, ½–1-inch diameter/1-foot circle of ¾-inch pine/wood preservative/drill

Drill a hole in the center of the circle large enough for the rope to fit through. Starting at 3 feet, place a knot in the rope every foot for approximately 3 more feet. Bring end of rope through hole and knot securely so the seat will not fall. Attach the other end of the rope to a tree or branch so that the swing is at child's level. Extra knots serve as handles for the child.

Tumbling Mats or Mattresses

Place old mattresses or second-hand gym mats well away from any rocks or hard objects. They may be used indoors or out for gymnastic feats.

Hammock

Children love riding together on a hammock, especially when it can be combined with a song. Supervision is needed since children eventually get overenthusiastic and try the 360-degree flip maneuver. At this point you may wish to climb aboard and read a quiet story accompanied by a gentle swing.

EXCURSIONS NEAR AND FAR

In the beginning of playgroup we found it best to restrict outings to the immediate surroundings. Visit a neighbor's beautiful garden or watch the workers at a construction site. As the year progresses and the children are more comfortable with each other, plan more extensive excursions. Such outings are great because they allow the children to mingle with their environment and enjoy each other's company. Before you embark on any excursion though, familiarize yourself with the surround-

ings. You can expect that some children in these new situations may feel the need to stay extra close to you. Here are some places we explored.

1. *Parents' Place of Employment.* This gives the children an opportunity to see different parents at different jobs.
2. *Bakery.* Arrange for a time when the children can observe the bakers preparing dough.
3. *Fire Station.* Contact your local station house for a demonstration of the equipment.
4. *Small Airport.* Check schedule for arrivals and departures of aircraft.
5. *Construction Sites.* Visit the site and watch the equipment being used. Name the different machines and talk about how they are being used.
6. *Library.* Story hour and films are usually scheduled for preschoolers throughout the year.
7. *Plant Stores, Greenhouses.* Discuss various plants and allow the children to choose a small plant to purchase and take home.
8. *Nature Trails, Arboretums, and Duck Ponds.* Explore wildlife areas in your neighborhood.

Note: Be sure to make use of any and all available community resources.

Winter Excursions

Window Shopping at Holiday Time. Cities and towns come alive with color during the holiday season. A brisk walk downtown followed by a hot chocolate at the local soda shop is bound to bring out the rosy cheeks.

Sledding. All you need is a small hill and some plastic mats or inner tubes for a snowy morning or afternoon of fun.

Sleigh Ride. If you live in a rural area, a local farm may offer sleigh rides through the woods. Check the yellow pages under sleigh or hay rides.

Ice Skating. This trip would require several adults. We had our children on double-runner skates at the age of two but there were lots of slips and spills.

Winter Walk. After a snowfall, exploring the tracks of small animals will fascinate the children.

Museums. Save visits to museums and libraries for inclement weather. The winters can be very long and you'll want to save some indoor excursions for those days.

Pet Store. This is a consistently successful winter indoor excursion. What glee the children express watching the puppies frolic in the store window.

Spring Excursions

Maple Sugar Camp. This is a wonderful experience if available in your territory. Watching the sap being gathered and smelling the luscious syrup boil in the sugar house enhances so many senses. Many places serve the treat "sugar on snow" (maple syrup on chipped ice).

Flowering Gardens. A local neighborhood garden in bloom makes a nice short excursion.

Duck Pond. Bring along some plastic bags of old bread to feed the ducks.

Farm. Many animals are born during the spring. Arrange ahead of time with the owners to ensure a successful trip to see them.

April Shower Walk. Make sure the children bring umbrella and boots, then have a great time slushing through the puddles. You also might need an extra set of clothing that day.

Bus Ride. A warm spring day is a great time for a trip downtown.

Spring Walk through the Woods. This is the time to show nature awakening after a long winter's rest.

Nursing Home. Everyone thinks of visiting the elderly at holiday time, but what about a visit from smiling preschoolers after a long cold winter?

Summer Excursions

Children's Outdoor Summer Theaters. Many local theater groups and college drama departments sponsor summer productions for children.

Picnics. A light lunch under a tree followed by swings and slides in the park is a perfect way to spend a summer's day.

Amusement Park. This excursion needs the supervision of several adults. Some larger parks have a small amusement area with simple, safe rides for the preschooler. We ended our playgroup year with a family outing at a small amusement area.

Berry-picking Area. Strawberry, raspberry, or blueberry picking at a local farm or just a small patch in a backyard followed by some homemade tarts is fun for all.

Animal Farms, Zoos. Small petting zoos allow maximal contact and minimal walking.

Vegetable Gardens. Late summer is just the right time to see ripening vegetables in neighborhood gardens.

Autumn Excursions

County or State Fairs. Since these events are usually quite large, it might be wise to see just a small part of the fair, for instance, the prizewinning livestock.

Apple Picking. Children pick and eat apples in one motion. Whatever is left over will make a great apple pie or applesauce.

Hiking. Combine exploring with a gathering expedition. Leaves, acorns, and other environmental goodies pasted to a display board make an autumn collage to bring home.

Pumpkin Patch. We knew a local farmer who allowed each child to choose any small pumpkin for ten cents. What a thrill!

Dried Flower Gathering. Roadside stands or local nurseries sell inexpensive dried flowers. These can be set in Styrofoam or clay to make a beautiful fall flower arrangement.

Craft Fairs and Bazaars. Many synagogues and churches sponsor bazaars and craft fairs this time of year. The kids will enjoy buying a used toy or small craft item at an inexpensive price.

12

GRAND FINALE

SIMPLE PROJECTS THEY'LL BE PROUD TO SHOW OFF

A project for preschoolers must be simple and structured. The best projects have a minimum number of steps. You'll need to guide the children through the various stages, giving specific instructions as they move along. It helps to go over the project first and have a copy of the finished project available. It's fun to coordinate your activities with holidays and seasons. Our kids had a great time creating their own Halloween costumes out of plain paper bags. It's very tempting for the parent to be over-involved. So keep in mind the ultimate aim—projects that are handmade by the children.

Try making some of these with your playgroup.

Pencil Holder

MATERIALS:

orange juice can/crayons/paper cut to the size of the can

Every studious preschooler needs a pencil holder, but it has to have a personal touch. So have the children color the precut paper and tape their drawings around the cans. Make sure the cans have no sharp edges. Cut fabric glued on works equally well and adds the personal touch. Youngsters take a special pride in what they make. Naomi never fails to notice her pencil holder on Grandma's desk when she visits. It was given two years ago.

Life-size Drawing

MATERIALS:

large sheets of paper/crayons

Large sheets of newsprint are great for life-size drawing. Have the children lie down and trace their figures. Let them color themselves, or if you are overloaded with old fabric let them "dress themselves," fastening their clothes with stapler or glue. You may wish to offer help with the features. Sometimes they'll include you and sometimes not.

Bird Nest Builder

MATERIALS:

wire mesh approximately 6 inches square/neutral yarn/pine needles/straw/masking tape

Here's a chance to help out our friendly neighbors the birds. Sometimes they run short on building material, so why not give them a hand in the springtime? Wrap the tape around the sharp wire edges. Have the children weave yarn, pine needles, and straw closely through the mesh. Attach a string to each of two corners for easy hanging. Have the children take the nest builder home to hang on their favorite tree. They will be able to observe the birds using the materials from the mesh to build their nests. Birds are afraid of bright colors, so for best results use natural-colored thread.

Paper Bag Puppet

MATERIALS:
crushed tissue or newspaper/paper sandwich bags/crayons/fabric/Magic Markers/yarn/sticks/tape

Puppets are lots of fun for preschoolers, and these are easy to make. Before you start, though, be sure to have an informal puppet stage ready. Just move your couch away from the wall so the kids can get behind it and use its top as a stage. Then with the children's help, crush the tissue or newspaper into balls. Have the children decorate the bags. You can use fabric, crayons, and Magic Markers liberally. Cut yarn makes nice hair. When your bags are beautiful, stuff them with the crushed paper. Place a large stick into the opening of the bag and secure it with lots of tape. Consider yourself the director as well as the producer. Whether it's a musical, drama, or soap opera is a choice you'll have to make!

Crazy Hats

MATERIALS:
crushed tissue/glue/large paper plates/heavy yarn or ribbon

Here's a jazzy one. Just glue this crushed tissue paper to the top of the plates. Now make two holes for the yarn or ribbon chin straps or use a stapler. Now on goes the music. Let the crazy dance begin.

Paper Bag Costumes

MATERIALS:

large and small supermarket bags/Magic Markers/glue/fabric/stapler

Time to make paper people or seasonal costume. Take a large bag and cut out holes for the arms and head so that the bag can easily slip over each child's head. Have the children decorate the costumes any way they wish. In addition, you can use smaller bags with openings for the eyes and mouth as a mask and coordinate it with the body. The result is the most fashionable collection of paper playgroupers you'll ever see. The decorations are up to you and the children. Just remember to decorate the costumes before they're on the children. It's much easier. If you're lucky enough to have a playgroup over on Halloween, dress them up and trick and treat at a few neighbors' homes.

Egg Carton Caterpillar

MATERIALS:

½ egg carton (cut the long way)/tempera paint/2 pieces of pipe cleaner/cotton balls

Caterpillars—fuzzy and yucky. Not this one! Here's a caterpillar even the shyest child will love. Just take an egg carton and ask the children to paint them in their best caterpillar colors. For you "touch enthusiasts" try pasting on some wisps of cotton for just the right feel. Then insert your two pipe cleaner antennas for the finishing touch. Now crawl, you caterpillars, but stay out of the living room.

Kite

MATERIALS:

large piece of construction paper/string/Magic Markers/cut straws/small square pieces of construction paper with a hole in the middle

Here's one for a windy day. Just cut a diamond shape out of a large piece of construction paper. Have the children decorate the shape. Make holes at two opposite points of the diamond. Tie a long string to one of the holes for the children to hold while the kite is flying. Tie a short string to the other hole for the tail. Assemble cut straws and other paper shapes with holes for the children to string on the tail. Tie a knot at the end so it all doesn't slip off. Now this kite won't last forever, but it will last long enough for a great morning run. And the nice thing is, they made it themselves.

Playgroup T-shirts

MATERIALS:

any T-shirt, preferably white, brought from home before playgroup meeting/fabric crayons that can be used directly on cloth (from any hobby craft shop)/iron/paper

"My big brother and sister have school shirts and sweaters, so why can't I?" Cheryl heard this over and over from Glen and decided to do something about it. Here it is. Before playgroup arrives, on the front of each T-shirt write a child's name with fabric crayons. Perhaps a smiley face in the middle will add to the design. Place a piece of paper over the design and press with an iron. When the children arrive, let them go to town on the back of the T-shirt. Press their design on the shirt. What could be greater than adding a playgroup T-shirt to their wardrobes? Ours were delighted with their creations and couldn't wait to wear them on playgroup day.

Leaf Press

MATERIALS:

wax paper sandwich bags/autumn leaves/iron

Here we have a little display case for your leaves, and it's easy too. Just have the children place their favorite leaves in the sandwich bags. It's hard to resist censoring their choice, but do resist. We'll never know what attracts some youngsters to brown crumbly leaves. Make sure that the leaves do not overlap. Press with a hot iron. Tape to a window for display.

Snow Figures

MATERIALS:

cotton balls or Styrofoam packing materials/glue/precut cardboard shapes

It's wintertime! Let's celebrate! Everyone loves the feel of cotton so give each child an ample supply. Help them make snowpeople with the aid of some glue and a Styrofoam plate. Use your imagination for accessories. If you want a real winner, try this. Before playgroup, cut out fabric figures, each with one arm outstretched. Give two to each child and paste one on either side of your plate. Now give them the cotton and let them create their own snowball fight. The "snow" may land anywhere on the plate.

Sponge Grass

MATERIALS:
shallow pans/ryegrass seed/cut sponges

Youngsters have a beautiful sense of priorities that includes a fascination with living things. Here's their chance to create life. Place each damp sponge into a shallow pan. Have the children sprinkle ryegrass seed on it. Let them take it home and water it frequently. They will be pleasantly surprised within a week as new life begins to pop out of an old sponge.

Carrot Top

MATERIALS:
carrot tops/shallow pans

Here's another chance to witness growth. Cut off a carrot top and place it in a shallow pan with a little water. Water every day and watch the roots and carrot tops grow. In preparation set up a little display of vegetables that grow above and below the ground. Explain how roots and leaves gather water to grow.

A HAPPY ENDING

Congratulations!! You made a commitment. You've set aside time for your child. And you've both become richer in many ways. There are a few extra fringe benefits you may have discovered along the way. Have you noticed how the playgroup has broadened your repertoire at home and seemed to stimulate activity with your other children and spouse? Were you surprised when your other kids asked you if they could help prepare that special project for their little brother's or sister's club? Wasn't it nice to see that your spouse was happy to have the kids visit work? Did you see how the playgroup tended to draw in the neighbors when you went outdoors—especially the older ones? Didn't the kids' smiles just brighten their day? And wasn't it great how the friendships grew strong? It sure came in handy during that family crisis when the kids needed a helping hand.

You didn't know you had it in you. But you did and you do! Your child is sure lucky to have you as a parent!!

RECOMMENDED READINGS

Gregg, Elizabeth. *What to Do When There's Nothing to Do.* Dell, New York, 1967. (An inexpensive paperback book with a variety of activities for children six months to five years of age.)

Lloyd, Janice, and Jean Marzallo. *Learning through Play.* Harper & Row, New York, 1978. (A compact paperback containing activities covering all aspects of a preschooler's development and growth.)

Marzallo, Jean. *Supertot.* Harper & Row, Colophon Books, New York, 1978. (A paperback book with unique activities for the young preschooler.)

Menlove, Coleen Kent. *Ready Set Go.* Prentice-Hall, Englewood Cliffs, New Jersey, 1978. (A paperback containing a variety of stimulating and clever activities to do with your preschooler.)

Peabody, Laura B., and Nancy Butterworth. *The Playgroup Handbook.* St. Martin's Press, New York, 1974. (A how-to book on conducting a playgroup with a variety of activities appropriate for each month.)

Porcher, Mary Ann, and Marie Winn. *The Playgroup Book.* Macmillan, New York, 1967. (Provides a variety of activities for three- and four-year-olds plus sound advice on organizing and conducting a playgroup.)

Sharp, Evelyn. *Thinking Is Child's Play.* Avon Books, New York, 1969. (Using a homemade set of shape and color cards, activities in thinking and problem solving are explored with your child.)

Winick, Mariann. *Before the 3 R's.* David McKay, New York, 1972. (A book containing simple activities to encourage development in skills such as size, color, and shape discrimination.)

INDEX

Acorns, 29
Activities
lack of interest in, 34
time scheduled for, 20
See also Art activities; Cooking activities; Dramatic activities; Gluing activities; Listening activities; Manipulative activities; Matching and classification activities; Musical activities; Outdoor activities; Painting activities; Projects; Size discrimination activities
Advertising, for playgroup participants, 15
Affection between children, 32
Age span of children in playgroup, 4, 19–20
Airport, visit to, 126
Amusement park, visit to, 128
Animal farm, visit to, 129
Animals
imitations of, 44
sorting pictures of, 76
See also Animal farm; Pet stores; Zoo
Apple picking, 129
Applesauce, homemade, 108
April shower walk, 128
Arboretum, visit to, 126
Art activities, finishing, 59
See also Creative activities; Painting; Sculpture
Art materials, checklist of, 21
Arts and crafts. *See* Projects
Auditory skills. *See* Listening activities
Autumn, excursions in, 129

Babies, and parents participation in playgroup, 15
Babysitters, 2–3, 4, 41
Bakers clay, recipe for, 52
Bakery
  dramatic activity, 47
  visit to, 126
Balance beam, 116–117
Ball Toss, 112
Banana Dunk Dip, 107
Banana-on-a-Stick, 102–103
Barber shop dramatic activity, 46–47
Bazaars. *See* Craft fairs and bazaars
Bean Bag Toss, 113
Beans in a Can, 55–56
Bedtime activities, finger plays as, 80
Behavior. *See* Negative behavior; Playing alone
Berry Delicious, 109
Berry-picking area, visit to, 129
Big and Little Game, 76
Bird nest builder, 132–133
Block printing, 67
Books
  on finger plays, 80
  on musical activities, 93–94
  on playgroup activities, 141–142
  for story telling, 95–100
Bottle Top Match, 75
Bottles, decorated as people, 75
Bread dough art, 52–53
Bulletin boards, and finding playgroup participants, 15
Buried logs, 122–123
Bus ride, 128
Button Sort, 74
Button Up, Zip Up, 57–58

Card games, 73
Card Sort, 75
Cardboard dolls, dressing, 62
Carrot top plant, 137
Carton, play stove made from, 26–27
Caterpillar, egg carton, 134
Cheese sandwiches, 108–109
Child/adult ratios, in childcare centers, 4
Child-care cooperatives. *See* Playgroups
Children
  and illness and injury, 40–41
  interactions and communication, 31–36
  participation in planned activities, 34
  playing alone, 32–33
  tracings of, 54, 132
Children's outdoor summer theaters, 128
Christmas
  decorations, 53
  window shopping before, 126–127
Cinnamon Toast, 106
Circle games. *See* Musical circle games

Clapping. *See* Rhythm clapping
Classification skills. *See* Matching and classification activities
Clay
  dried flowers in, 129
  excess, 25
  See also Bakers clay; "Play Dough"
Cleaning up, storage containers and, 24
Clothing. *See* Used clothing
Color discrimination activities, 69
  and "If You're Wearing. . ." circle game, 91
  and "I'm Selling Lollipops" circle game, 91–92
  and Pattern Sort, 74–75
Coloring, 54
Communication learning, 31–36
  dramatic activities and, 43–48
Community resources
  excursions and, 126
  materials for outdoor play equipment and, 115–116
  for playgroup materials, 24–28
  and recycling center, 29
Computer paper, 28
Construction site, visit to, 125, 126
Cookie Paint — Variation 1, 104–105
Cookie Paint — Variation 2, 105
Cookies
  and play dough, 52
  recipes for, 103–105
Cooking activities, 101–109
  applesauce, 108
  Banana Dunk Dip, 107
  Banana-on-a-Stick, 102–103
  Berry Delicious, 109
  cheese sandwiches, 108–109
  cinnamon toast, 106
  Cookie Paint — Variation 1, 104–105
  Cookie Paint — Variation 2, 105
  Easy Roll-Out Cookie Dough, 104
  Graham Cracker No-Bake Cookies, 104
  Jell-O Shapes, 105–106
  No-Bake Cookies — Variation 1, 103
  No-Bake Cookies — Variation 2, 103–104
  One-Rise Buttermilk Bread, 107–108
  Orange Delight, 109
  peanut butter, 106–107
  peanut butter cookies, 105
  popcorn, 106
  Roll-Pat Cookies, 103
  stuffed celery, 107
Coordination
  and rope jump, 113
  See also Manipulative activities

Costumes, 43
  paper bag, 134
Craft fairs and bazaars, visits to, 129
Crazy Hats, 133
Creative activities. *See* Gluing activities; Painting; Projects; Sculpting
Criticism of children, 33
Crying, 32, 37
Cutting activities, 51
Cymbals, 85

Dances, Scarf and Streamer, 86
Dexterity, development of, 49
  See also Manipulative activities
Diaper changes, parents' attitudes toward, 28-29
Discipline, 33-34
  discussions at preplaygroup visits on, 38
  selection of parent participants and, 16, 17
  See also Physical punishment
Doctor dramatic activity, 46
Dramatic activities
  bakery, 47
  barber shop, 46-47
  equipment for, 43
  finger plays, 79-82
  Fire! Fire!, 44-45
  Is There a Doctor in the House? 46
  party time, 48
  post office, 47
  supermarket, 45-46
  and 3-D glued sets, 65
  zoo trip, 44
Dramatic activities materials, checklist for, 21
Dried flower gathering, 129
Drums, 84
Duck pond, visit to, 126, 128

Easy Roll-Out Cookie Dough, 104
Egg carton caterpillar, 134
Electrical wire telephone company spools, for outdoor play equipment, 115, 118-122
Elevated walkway, 120-121
Employment, playgroup participation by parents and, 12-14
Environmental activities. *See* Outdoor activities
Environment of playgroup. *See* Physical environment; Social environment
Environmental gluing, 62-63
Equipment
  basic checklist, 21-22
  See also Materials; Outdoor equipment; Recyclable materials
Excursions, 125-129
  in autumn, 129
  in spring, 127-128
  in summer, 128-129
  in winter, 126-127
Extended family, lack of, 1, 7
Eyedropper painting, 68

Eye-hand coordination
manipulative activities and, 49-50
pouring water and, 112

Fabric gluing, 61-62
Fabric scraps, 28
Fairs, county or state, visit to, 129
"Farmer in the Dell, The," 87-88
Farms
visit to, 128
and Where Do They Live? activity, 76
Fatigue, reaction to, 35-36
Feather painting, 70
Film containers, 25
Finger painting, 65-66
Finger plays, 79-82
Fire! Fire!, 44-45
"Fire starter" paper balls, 57
Fire station, visit to, 126
Fireman dramatic activity, 44-45
Fishnet or rope-mesh climbers, 123
Flexibility
of playgroup routine, 34-35
and selection of parent participants, 18
Flowering gardens, visits to, 127
Furniture
checklist, 22
protection during painting, 66

Games, homemade. *See* Matching and classification activities
Gardening, 113-114
Gardens, visits to, 125, 127
Geo-boards, 55
Gluing activities
crumbled tissue gluing, 60-61
demonstration by parent, 59
environmental object gluing, 24, 62-63
fabric gluing, 61-62
hard and soft objects gluing, 61
paper gluing, 62
sand gluing, 63-64
3-D gluing, 64-65
wallpaper gluing, 64
Going home time, dressing at, 58
Graham Cracker No-Bake Cookies, 104
Group toys, parent involvement in sharing of, 37-38

Halloween
costumes for, 131
decorations for, 53
Hammock, 124
Hard and soft objects gluing, 61
Hay rides, 127
"Here We Go Looby Loo," 88
Hiking, 129
Hobbyhorse Fin, 86-87
Homes for playgroups, suitability of, 14-15

Host child, special jobs for, 36
Household items, for play-group material, 23–24

"Ice-cream cones," from colored sand, 63–64
Ice skating, 127
"If You're Wearing..." 91
Illness
  of children, 40
  of parent in charge, 40
Imagination. *See* Dramatic activities
"I'm a Little Teapot," 92
"I'm Selling Lollipops," 91–92
Imitation, finger plays and, 79–82
Indian bead necklaces, 53
Individual differences
  activity planning and, 34
  advantages of, 39
  behavior and, 33–34
  manipulative activities and, 49
  reaction to fatigue and, 35–36
Is There a Doctor in the House? dramatic activity, 46

Jell-O Shapes, 105–106
Job site of parent, visit to, 126, 139
Junk. *See* Recyclable materials
"Junk art." *See* Gluing activities

Kitchen timer, toy sharing and, 36–37
Kite, 135
Language learning, dramatic play and, 44
Language materials, checklist of, 22
Leaf press, 136
Leather scraps, 25
Leaves, 29
  display case for, 136
Library, visit to, 126
Life-size drawings, 54, 132
Likenesses and differences, recognition of. *See* Matching and classification activities
Listening activities, 79–100
  finger plays, 79–82
  See also Music; Story telling
Lotto games, 73

Magazine pictures, 62
Magic tricks, sponges and, 68
Manipulative activities, 49–58
  Beans in a Can, 55–56
  bread dough art, 52–53
  Button Up, Zip Up, 57–58
  coloring, 54
  cutting, 51
  Geo-Boards, 55
  Nuts and Bolts, 56
  Paper Crunch, 57
  Rings and Hooks, 54–55
  sewing, 53–54
  stringing, 53
  water play fun, 56–57
  See also Manipulative materials
Manipulative materials
  checklist for, 21
  "Play Dough," 51–52

Maple sugar camp, visit to, 127
Marble painting, 71
Marching, 86
Matching and classification activity, 73-77
  Big and Little Game, 76
  Bottle Top Match, 75
  Button Sort, 74
  Card Sort, 75
  Pattern Sort, 74-75
  Shape Match, 73-74
  Size Game, 77
  Touch Game, 77
  Wallpaper Match, 75-76
  What Belongs in the Room? 77
  Where Do They Live? 76
Materials
  for dramatic activities, 43
  for matching and classification activities, 73
  from outdoors, 28-29
  See also Equipment; Manipulative materials; Outdoor equipment
Merchants, donations of collectibles, 24-28
  See also Community resources
Messiness
  and art activities, 59, 65
  parents' reactions to, 17, 18
Metal play equipment, 114-115
Monkey seat, 123-124
"Muffin Man," 92-93
"Mulberry Bush, The," 89-90
Mural painting, 69-70
Museums, visits to, 127
Music
  during feather painting, 70
  See also Musical activities; Musical circle games; Musical instruments; Musical movement; Records
Musical activities
  books on, 93, 94
  Crazy Hats for, 133
Musical circle games
  "Farmer in the Dell, The," 87-88
  "Here We Go Looby Loo," 88
  "I'm Selling Lollipops," 91-92
  "If You're Wearing. . ." 91
  "I'm a Little Teapot," 92
  "Muffin Man," 92-93
  "Mulberry Bush," 89-90
  "Ring around the Rosy," 89
Musical instruments, homemade, 82-85
  cymbals, 85
  drums, 84
  rhythm sticks, 84
  sandblocks, 84-85
  shakers, 82-83
Musical materials, checklist for, 22
Musical movement, 86-87
  Hobbyhorse Fun, 86-87
  marching, 86
  Rhythm Clapping, 86
  Scarf and Streamer Dancing, 86

Nature trails, visit to, 126
Negative behavior of children, 33
No-Bake Cookies — Variation 1, 103
No-Bake Cookies — Variation 2, 103–104
Number recognition, Card Sort and, 75
Nursery school, playgroup as preparation for, 8–9
Nursing home, visit to, 128
Nuts and Bolts, 56

Observation of parent-child interactions,
  selection of playgroup participants and, 16–17
Observation skills. *See* Cooking activities
Old clothes. *See* Used clothing
One-Rise Buttermilk Bread, 107–108
Orange Delight, 109
Outdoor activities, 111–129
  Ball Toss, 112
  Bean Bag Toss, 113
  gardening, 113–114
  Hula Hoop Jump, 113
  indoors activities outside, 111
  Rope Jump, 113
  sand play, 111–112
  scheduling of, 111
  water painting, 114
  water play, 112
  in winter, 92
  See also Excursions; Outdoor play equipment
Outdoor play equipment, 114–124
  balance beam, 116–117
  buried logs, 122–123
  checklist for, 22
  elevated walkway, 120–121
  fishnet or rope-mesh climbers, 123
  hammock, 124
  monkey seat or rope seat, 123–124
  spool bridge, 119
  spool fort, 120
  spool slide, 121–122
  spool table and chairs, 118
  tire sandbox, 118
  tire swing, 117–118
  tire tunnel, 118
  tumbling mats or mattresses, 124

Packing materials, 26
Painting activities
  block printing, 67
  eyedropper painting, 78
  feather painting, 70
  finger painting, 65–66
  marble painting, 71
  mural painting, 69–70
  Q-Tip painting, 72
  rock painting, 70–71
  sponge painting, 66–67
  straw painting, 71
  and tempera, *see* Tempera
  texture painting, 67–68
  watercolor painting, 69

See also Water painting
Paper
computer, 28
for finger painting, 65
Paper bag costumes, 134
Paper bag puppet, 133
Paper Crunch, 57
Paper gluing, 62
Paperweights, painted rock, 71
Parades. *See* Marching
Parent-child interactions, selection of playgroup participants and, 16
Parents
ability to work with playgroup, 11-12
benefits of playgroups and, 139
communication among, 38-41
illness of, 40
involvement in group play, 37-38
and negative traits of children, 33-34
reaction to child's problem, 39
relationships between, 8
social behavior with children, 32
role in art activity teaching, 59
See also Participants in playgroup
Participants in playgroup
meeting of, 18-19
qualifications of, 11-12
and scheduling problems, 12-14
selection of, 15-18, 19
with small babies, 15
suitability of home, 14-15
Party time dramatic activity, 48
Pattern Sort, 74-75
Peanut Butter Cookies, 105
Peanut butter, homemade, 106-107
Peer involvement, playgroups and, 1-2
Pencil holder, 131-132
Pencils and crayons, holding, 49-50
Personality clashes, 39
Pet store, visit to, 127
Physical environment, materials from, 21-29
Physical punishment, 34
Picnics, 128
Pinecones, 29
Plant stores and greenhouses, visit to, 126
"Play dough," homemade, 51-52
Play stove, homemade, 26-27
Playing alone, 32-33
Playgroup
advantages of, 4-9
common misgivings about, 11-15
defined, 3-4
early meetings of, 19
equipment checklist of, 21-22
fringe benefits of, 139

guidelines for success of, 19-20
and parental understanding of childhood behavior, 40
as preparation for nursery school, 8-9
reasons for organizing, 1-3
recommended reading on, 141-142
schedules for, 12-14, 18-19, 20
See also Participants in playgroup
Playgroup T-shirts, 135-136
Playhouse, refrigerator carton, 26
Popcorn, 106
Post office dramatic activity, 47
Preplaygroup visits, 38-39
Pretending. *See* Dramatic activities
Printing, block printing activity and, 67
Projects, 131-137
bird nest builder, 132-133
carrot top plant, 137
Crazy Hats, 133
egg carton caterpillar, 134
kite, 135
leaf press, 136
life-size drawing, 132
paper bag costumes, 134
paper bag puppet, 133
pencil holder, 131-132
playgroup T-shirts, 135-136
snow figures, 136
sponge grass, 137
Pumpkin patch, visit to, 129
Pumpkins, clay, 53
Punishment. *See* Discipline
Puppets, paper bag, 133

Q-Tip painting, 72
Quarrels, 34

Reading, matching and classification skills and, 73
Records, 85
train, 43-44
Recyclable materials, 23-29
from community resources, 24-28
household items, 23-24
Recycling centers, 29
Refrigerator cartons, playhouse from, 26
Responsibility, rotation of, 19
Rhythm Clapping, 86
Rhythm sticks, 84
"Ring around the Rosy," 89
Rings and Hooks, 54-55
Rock painting, 70-71
Rocks, 29
Roll-Pat Cookies, 103
Rope Jump, 113
Rope seat, 123-124
Rubber bands, and Geo-Boards, 55

Safety, outdoor play equipment and, 116
Sand, under outdoor play equipment, 116
Sand gluing, 63-64
Sand play, 111-112

Sandblocks, 84-85
Sandbox, 111-112
  See also Tire sandbox
Scarf and Streamer Dancing, 86
Science, art and, 68
Screaming, 35-36
Sculpting
  bread dough art, 52-53
  "Play Dough" and, 51-52
Seashells, 29
Security, positive behavior and, 32
Separation from mother, 9, 32
Sewing, 53-54
Shakers, 25, 82-83
Shape Match, 73-74
Sharing, 36-38
  cooking activities and, 101
Shopping. *See* Supermarket dramatic activity
Shy children, 34
Size discrimination activities, 55
  Big and Little Game, 76
  Nuts and Bolts, 56
  Size Game, 77
Size Game, 77
Sledding, 127
Sleigh rides, 127
Snow figures, 136
Social environment
  communication among parents and, 38-41
  communication learning and, 31-36
  mural painting and, 70
  and sharing, 36-38
Sorting. *See* Matching and classification activities
Spatial form, eyedropper painting and, 68
Spills. *See* Messiness
Sponge grass, 137
Sponge painting, 66-67
Sponges, water disappearing trick with, 68
Spool bridge, 119
Spool fort, 120
Spool slide, 121-122
Spool table and chairs, 118
Spring, excursions in, 127-128
Storage containers
  checklist for, 22
  homemade, 24
Stories
  for color learning, 69
  on found objects, 63
  See also Story telling
Story telling
  choice of books for, 95-96
  in hammock, 124
  list of books for, 96-100
  method, 94-95
Stove. *See* Play stove
Straw painting, 71
Stringing, 53
Stuffed celery, 107
Styrofoam, 25-26
  dried flowers in, 129
Summer, excursions in, 128-129

Telephone numbers, 40-41
Telephone wire spools, 27-28, 115, 118-122

Tempera paint, 66
  and feather painting, 70
  and marble painting, 71
  and mural painting, 69-70
  and Q-Tip painting, 72
  and rock painting, 70-71
  and straw painting, 71
Texture discrimination, Touch Game and, 77
Texture painting, 67-68
Theaters. *See* Children's outdoor summer theaters
3-D gluing, 64-65
Thrift shops, 73
Thumbprinting, 66
Tire sandbox, 118
Tire swing, 117-118
Tire tunnel, 118
Tires, for outdoor play equipment, 116, 117-118
Tissue paper, gluing, 60-61
Touch Game, 77
Toys, sharing, 36-38
Tracings of children, 54, 132
Train ride, imaginary, 43-44
T-shirts, playgroup, 135-136
Tumbling mats or mattresses, 124
Two-year-olds, social skills of, 31

Used clothing, 43, 57-58

Valentine's Day decorations, 53
Vegetable gardens, visit to, 129
Verbal skills, dramatic activities and, 43
Visual discrimination materials, checklist for, 21

Walks
  during April shower, 128
  to find gluing objects, 62-63
  in winter, 127
  in woods, 128
  See also Hiking
Wallpaper books, 24-25
Wallpaper gluing, 64
Wallpaper Match, 75-76
Water painting, 114
Water play, 56-57, 112
Watercolor painting, 69
What Belongs in the Room? 77
Where Do They Live? 76
Window shopping, 126-127
Winter, excursions in, 126-127
Wood chips, 25
Woods
  sleigh ride through, 127
  walk through, 128
Workplaces. *See* Job sites
Writing, prerequisites for, 49-50

Yarn scraps, 28

Zippers. *See* Button Up, Zip Up
Zoos
  visits to, 44, 129
  and Where Do They Live? activity, 76